TRAEGER WOOD PELLET GRILL AND SMOKER COOKBOOK FOR BEGINNERS

200 COMPLETE AND DELICIOUS BBQ RECIPES TO MASTER YOUR TRAEGER WOOD PELLET GRILL AND SMOKER EASILY

SHEILA FRENCH

Copyright © 2021 by Sheila French- All rights reserved.

The content contained within this book may not be reproduced, duplicated, or transmitted without direct written permission from the author or the publisher. Under no circumstances will any blame or legal responsibility be held against the publisher, or author, for any damages, reparation, or monetary loss due to the information contained within this book, either directly or indirectly.

Legal Notice: This book is copyright protected. It is only for personal use. You cannot amend, distribute, sell, use, quote or paraphrase any part, or the content within this book, without the consent of the author or publisher.

Disclaimer Notice: Please note the information contained within this document is for educational and entertainment purposes only. All effort has been executed to present accurate, up to date, reliable, complete information. No warranties of any kind are declared or implied. Readers acknowledge that the author is not engaged in the rendering of legal, financial, medical, or professional advice. The content within this book has been derived from various sources. Please consult a licensed professional before attempting any techniques outlined in this book. By reading this document, the reader agrees that under no circumstances is the author responsible for any losses, direct or indirect, that are incurred as a result of the use of the information contained within this document, including, but not limited to, errors, omissions, or inaccuracies.

CONTENTS

INTRODUCTION 10
- How Your Traeger Wood Pellet Grill Works 10
- Seeing the Benefits of Your Traeger Wood Pellet Grill 10
- Better to Use Your Wood Pellet Grill 11
- Cleaning Tricks for Your Traeger Wood Pellet Grill 14

BAKING RECIPES 15
- Smoky Apple Crepes 15
- Mexican Black Bean Cornbread Casserole 15
- Marbled Brownies With Amaretto & Ricotta 16
- Savory Cheesecake With Bourbon Pecan Topping 16
- Caramelized Bourbon Baked Pears 17
- Pumpkin Bread 18
- Bacon Chocolate Chip Cookies 18
- Delicious Pellet Grill Cornbread 19
- Ultimate Baked Garlic Bread 19
- Baked Bourbon Maple Pumpkin Pie 20
- Spiced Lemon Cherry Pie 21
- Smoky Pimento Cheese Cornbread 21
- Mint Butter Chocolate Chip Cookies 22
- Eggs Ham Benedict 22
- Skillet Buttermilk Cornbread 23
- Green Bean Casserole Circa 1955 23
- Baked Pumpkin Pie 23
- Grilled Bourbon Pecan Pie 24
- Smoked Blackberry Pie 24
- Sweet And Spicy Baked Pork Beans 25
- Dark Chocolate Brownies With Bacon-salted Caramel 25
- Chocolate Lava Cake With Smoked Whipped Cream 26
- Sourdough Pizza 26
- Rosemary Cranberry Apple Sage Stuffing 27

    Pull-apart Dinner Rolls 27

    Donut Bread Pudding 28

SEAFOOD RECIPES 29

    Smoked Honey Salmon 29

    Delicious Smoked Trout 29

    Garlic Pepper Shrimp Pesto Bruschetta 29

    Traeger Smoked Salmon 30

    Barbecued Shrimp 30

    Teriyaki Smoked Honey Tilapia 31

    Smoked Cedar Plank Salmon 31

    Cedar Smoked Garlic Salmon 31

    Garlic Bacon Wrapped Shrimp 32

    Coconut Shrimp Jalapeño Poppers 32

    Charleston Crab Cakes With Remoulade 33

    Grilled Lemon Lobster Tails 34

    Grilled Whole Steelhead Fillet 34

    Smoke-roasted Halibut With Mixed Herb Vinaigrette 35

    Spicy Lime Shrimp 35

    Grilled Lobster Tails With Smoked Paprika Butter 36

    Salmon Cakes With Homemade Tartar Sauce 36

    Grilled Albacore Tuna With Potato-tomato Casserole 37

    Baked Whole Fish In Sea Salt 37

    Oysters In The Shell 37

    Lobster Tail 38

    Grilled Blackened Saskatchewan Salmon 38

    Sweet Smoked Salmon Jerky 38

    Honey Balsamic Salmon 39

    Spicy Crab Poppers 39

PORK RECIPES 40

    Whiskey- & Cider-brined Pork Shoulder 40

    Pork Tenderloin 40

    Bbq Sweet & Smoky Ribs 41

    Spiced Pulled Pork Shoulder 42

Smoked Bacon Roses 42
Grilled Sweet Pork Tenderloin 43
Pickle Brined Grilled Pork Chops 43
Sweet And Spicy Pork Roast 43
Apple-smoked Pork Tenderloin 44
Bbq Breakfast Grits 44
Smoked Rendezvous Ribs 44
Grilled Raspberry Chipotle Pork Ribs 45
Onion Pork Shoulder 45
Smoked Chili Con Queso By Doug Scheiding 46
Pork Belly Burnt Ends 47
St. Louis Bbq Ribs 47
Anytime Pork Roast 47
Apple Bacon Smoked Ham 48
Smoked Pig Shots 49
Grilled Pork Belly 49
3-2-1 Spare Ribs 49
Baked Candied Bacon Cinnamon Rolls 50
Balsamic Brussels Sprouts With Bacon 50
Southern Sugar-glazed Ham 51
Smoked Pork Loin With Sauerkraut And Apples 51
Smoked Ham 52

VEGETABLES RECIPES 53
Smoked Jalapeño Poppers 53
Roasted Do-ahead Mashed Potatoes 53
Baked Stuffed Avocados 54
Roasted Asparagus 54
Butternut Squash 54
Roasted Sweet Potato Steak Fries 54
Grilled Asparagus And Spinach Salad 55
Grilled Broccoli Rabe 55
Mashed Red Potatoes 56
Roasted Tomatoes With Hot Pepper Sauce 56

Baked Artichoke Parmesan Mushrooms 56
Smoked Beet-pickled Eggs 57
Double-smoked Cheese Potatoes 57
Roasted Fall Vegetables 58
Roasted Red Pepper White Bean Dip 59
Grilled Street Corn 59
Green Bean Casserole 60
Grilled Asparagus & Honey-glazed Carrots 60
Roasted New Potatoes With Compound Butter 60
Sicilian Stuffed Mushrooms 61
Smoked Mushrooms 62
Smoked & Loaded Baked Potato 62
Grilled Corn On The Cob With Parmesan And Garlic 62
Tater Tot Bake 63
Skillet Potato Cake 63
Baked Breakfast Mini Quiches 64

POULTRY RECIPES 65
Spiced Bbq Turkey 65
Chicken Breast Calzones 65
Beer Chicken 66
Cajun Brined Maple Smoked Turkey Breast 66
Roasted Honey Bourbon Glazed Turkey 67
Delicious Smoked Turketta 67
Glazed Bbq Half Chicken 67
Bbq Spatchcocked Chicken 68
Italian Grilled Barbecue Chicken Wings 68
Bbq Cheese Chicken Stuffed Bell Peppers 69
Fig Glazed Chicken Stuffed Cornbread 69
Smoked Buffalo Fries 70
Bbq Chicken Tostada 70
Smoked Cheesy Chicken Quesadilla 71
Teriyaki Apple Cider Turkey 72
Smoked Whole Chicken 72

Oktoberfest Pretzel Mustard Chicken ... 73
Grilled Beantown Chicken Wings ... 73
Smoked Wings ... 74
Cider-brined Turkey ... 74
Bbq Chicken Breasts ... 75
Spicy Bbq Whole Chicken ... 75
Grilled Honey Chicken Kabobs ... 76
Big Game Roast Chicken ... 76
Baked Prosciutto-wrapped Chicken Breast With Spinach And Boursin ... 76
Grilled Honey Garlic Wings ... 77

APPETIZERS AND SNACKS ... 78

Chicken Wings With Teriyaki Glaze ... 78
Bacon-wrapped Jalapeño Poppers ... 78
Bacon Pork Pinwheels (kansas Lollipops) ... 79
Bayou Wings With Cajun Rémoulade ... 79
Pulled Pork Loaded Nachos ... 80
Citrus-infused Marinated Olives ... 81
Chorizo Queso Fundido ... 81
Grilled Guacamole ... 82
Pigs In A Blanket ... 83
Simple Cream Cheese Sausage Balls ... 83
Deviled Eggs With Smoked Paprika ... 83
Smoked Cashews ... 84
Pig Pops (sweet-hot Bacon On A Stick) ... 85
Chuckwagon Beef Jerky ... 85
Smoked Cheese ... 86
Roasted Red Pepper Dip ... 86
Delicious Deviled Crab Appetizer ... 87
Smoked Turkey Sandwich ... 88
Sriracha & Maple Cashews ... 88
Jalapeño Poppers With Chipotle Sour Cream ... 88
Cold-smoked Cheese ... 89

COCKTAILS RECIPES ... 91

Smoked Eggnog 91
Garden Gimlet Cocktail 91
Strawberry Mule Cocktail 92
Bacon Old-fashioned Cocktail 92
Smoked Ice Mojito Slurpee 92
Smoked Hibiscus Sparkler 93
Traeger Gin & Tonic 93
Grilled Peach Smash Cocktail 94
Smoked Pineapple Hotel Nacional Cocktail 94
Smoke And Bubz Cocktail 95
Traeger Old Fashioned 95
Grilled Peach Sour Cocktail 95
A Smoking Classic Cocktail 96
Grilled Hawaiian Sour 96
Grilled Blood Orange Mimosa 96
Batter Up Cocktail 97
Smoked Hot Buttered Rum 97
Smoked Plum And Thyme Fizz Cocktail 97
Smoked Irish Coffee 98
Smoked Grape Lime Rickey 98
Traeger Smoked Daiquiri 99
Fig Slider Cocktail 99
Smoked Berry Cocktail 100
Grilled Peach Mint Julep 100
Smoking Gun Cocktail 101
Smoked Salted Caramel White Russian 101

BEEF LAMB AND GAME RECIPES 102
Smoked Meatball Egg Sandwiches 102
Dry Brined Texas Beef Ribs By Doug Scheiding 102
Beef Tenderloin With Tomato Vinaigrette 103
Irish Pasties 103
Smoked Tri-tip 104
Bbq Burnt End Sandwich 104

Citrus Grilled Lamb Chops	105
Sweet Heat Burnt Ends	105
Smoked Pheasant	106
Naked Juicy Lucy Burgers With Special Sauce	106
Philly Cheese Onion Steaks	107
Sweetheart Steak	108
Cornish Game In Mandarin Glaze	108
Beef Brisket With Chophouse Steak Rub	109
Fajita Style Mexican Hot Dogs	109
Spiced Lamb Burgers With Tzatziki	109
Flavour Bbq Brisket Burnt Ends	110
Bourbon Beef And Pork Meatballs	110
Roasted Elk Jalapeno Poppers	111
Smoked Pot Roast Brisket	111
Beef Caldereta Stew	112
Garlic Prime Rib Roast	112
Grilled Lemon Skirt Steak	113
Traeger Smoked Salami	113

INTRODUCTION

How Your Traeger Wood Pellet Grill Works

The name itself refers to the method of heating. Pellet grills use a different fuel to traditional grills (which rely upon sources like charcoal or gas)–they use up and burn wooden pellets. These wooden pellets look like little tablets or tiny rolled cigars; they're actually just compressed sawdust.

These wooden pellets are rotated into the fire pot, where they are exposed to intense heat, combust and emit heat and smoke of their own. This process is stoked by an internal fan, which then sends and distributes the heat throughout the grill. As you can see, this is a different method of heating–almost a combination of traditional ovens and flame cooking.

The method of cooking is called convection heating, which is the same method used by traditional smoke boxes.

The advantage of this is that the food is separated from the fire by a metal plate–which means there are no flare-ups and no grease falls into the fire pit (which can, in turn, burn up and produce an unwelcome flavor, along with being a pain to clean).

Seeing the Benefits of Your Traeger Wood Pellet Grill

1. Easy To Manage Temperature

One of biggest obstacles people have when it comes to grilling and smoking meats is getting the fire started and controlling the temperatures.

If folks want to use a charcoal grill then they deal with getting the charcoal lit, adjusting the vents, waiting for temperatures to stabilize, adding more fuel during a cook, etc. If they are using a gas grill then getting it lit is easy but dialing in a temperature is difficult. Gas grills are designed for Low, Medium and High. What exactly those settings means is going to depend upon your grill, the ambient weather, etc.

Dealing with temperature control is the problem that dives so many people to using electric smokers where they can just dial in a temperature, sit back and relax.

When it comes to temperature control, using a pellet smoker is just as easy as using an electric smoker! You dial in a temperature, wait 15-20 minutes for the grill to stabilize and then start grilling!

2. Flavor Is An Upgrade Over Electric And Propane

Without question, meat cooked on a pellet grill tastes better than meat cooked with an electric smoker or on a gas grill.

When you use an electric smoker the smoke flavor comes from smoldering wood chips that have to be replenished throughout the cook. When you are cooking on a pellet grill the smoke comes from the continually burning wood. The smoke from burning wood smells and tastes better than that from smoldering wood and gives a better smoke ring to boot. Same goes for meat cooked on a gas grill or smoker.

3. Minimal Flare Ups

The basic design of almost all pellet grills places shields between the flames in the fire pot and the dripping grease. This design has the intrinsic benefit of reducing flare ups to just about zero.

If you have been grilling on a cheap gas grill or directly over lit charcoal then you know that if you are not paying attention then a sudden flare up can happen and scorch whatever you are cooking.

4. Relatively Large Capacity

It doesn't cost much more money for a manufacturer to produce a large pellet grill vs a small one. The core expenses of the stand, electronics, auger, fan, smoke stack, pellet hopper, etc are constant. The only difference is making the cook chamber a little longer and the grates a little bigger.

Better to Use Your Wood Pellet Grill

1. Use Your Pellet Grill Like You Use Your Oven

One of the simplest and best tricks I have learned is to use your pellet grill like you use your oven.

Not every food is great with smoke added, but most things are! So experiment.

Any recipe that calls for roasting or baking in your kitchen oven can be transferred to your pellet smoker, simply by cooking for the same length of time and at the same temperature.

2. Use a Thermometer, Not Your Clock

Following on from the above oven tip, using a thermometer to gauge the internal temperatures of your meat will ensure a better cook rather than using time alone.

After all, it might have been cooking for the suggested time, but if it doesn't reach the right temperature inside, you could severely overcook your food. Or worse, undercook it and make yourself and your guests very ill.

Using a thermometer will also save you from opening the cooking chamber, just to keep checking on the progress of your meat.

The saying goes 'if you're looking, you ain't cooking!'. This is because as you open the door, you let all the heat escape, preventing all that hot smokey goodness from progressing the cook.

So, if your pellet smoker doesn't come with an integrated thermometer, we recommend investing in a good quality, 3rd party digital one. This way, you can monitor the cook via your thermometer and let the grill do its thing!

3. Use Those Upper Racks

Not only do upper racks give you extra space inside your grill, but they also mean the meat you've placed on them is further from the heat source.

This means the meat is being cooked more by convection, rather than radiant heat, which offers a more even cook.

Utilize every space and rack you have, and you'll also get more bang for your buck with the wood pellets you burn, as well as have a lot more food to go around!

4. Get Your Reverse Searing On

To sear or reverse sear? That is the question! But know that pellet grills are brilliant at reverse searing your meat, and not enough grillers do it!

To get that medium-rare finish edge to edge, with a perfectly seared smokey edge, we recommend you learn how to reverse sear.

Think of this process, almost like sous vide cooking. You create the perfect finish throughout the entire steak that you are looking for, cooking with a very low and gentle heat, to ensure none of it, not even the surface, is overcooked.

Only after reaching the perfect doneness throughout, do you then sear to create the Maillard crust and caramelized edge that creates a succulent sensory experience on top of that tender meat.

Depending on the model of your pellet grill and what you're cooking, set your grill temperature to 225f and place your meat in.

Once the internal temperature of your meat reaches 125f, which typically takes 45 minutes to an hour for a 2" thick steak (for medium-rare), take your meat out.

Crank up the grill to 500f, allowing it to heat through thoroughly, and then move the meat back into the grill, on a lower rack, and sear it for a couple of minutes with the lid closed, turning it once, until you have a great crust.

The result will be perfectly medium-rare meat throughout, with a great crust. And not a hint of that grey, overcooked outer edge you often get with the traditional sear.

5. Creating a Smokier Flavor

This tip is for those larger cuts of meat that you want to pull more smoke into, such as beef brisket or a chuck roast.

Smoke loves cold meats, 'condensing' onto the surface more readily than it does to warm surfaces. So the colder it is, the more chance you'll give the smoke to adhere to it.

So, instead of allowing your meat to come up to room temperature – as many recipes request you to do – whip it straight out of the fridge with the dry rub you placed on it the night before and put it straight into the pellet smoker.

As usual, set it to a low smoking temperature and allow it that extra time with the smoke, to get a more pronounced smoke flavor.

Cleaning Tricks for Your Traeger Wood Pellet Grill

1. Burning Off the Grill after Grilling

Depends on how much gunk/food residue is left, I like to give the grill a good brush down, then fire up to max temperature for 5 minutes. Then a follow up brushing and turning off/cooling down sequence.

2. Grill Cleaning a Few Options

You can just go for a wire brush (check that you pellet grill grill can handle an abrasive brush, some can, some can't) or get a specific tool that is a bit more thorough, design specific.

TIP: If you don't have either of these tools, you can use a scrunched up bit of tin foil to clean in between the grates.

If your not into cleaning the pellet grill after each cook, a minimum of cleaning after each 40 lb of pellets should be done.

3. Ash Removal After Each Cook

Once off and cool I take the ash out, do a quick check inside to see if there is any grease build up.

Even though there won't be much, I like to always empty the ash after a cook.

Getting rid of the ash is always a good idea after each cook, and some pellet grills like the Campchef's have simple pull out knobs for ash removal.

4. Clean Probe In Pellet Grill

The internal temperature probe, once cooled, should have a wipe.

A small amount of vinegar and water, with a scourer or scrubber, is an easy technique to keep the probe clean.

BAKING RECIPES

Smoky Apple Crepes

Servings: 6
Cooking Time: 60 Minutes

Ingredients:
- 1/2 Cup Apple Juice
- 2 Lbs Apples
- 2 Tbsp Brown Sugar
- 5 Tbsp Butter
- 3 Tbsp Butter, Melted
- Tt Caramel
- 3/4 Tsp Cinnamon, Ground
- Tt Cinnamon-Sugar
- 3/4 Tsp Cornstarch
- 2 Eggs
- 1 Cup Flour
- 2 Tsp Lemon Juice
- Tennessee Apple Butter Seasoning
- 1/2 Cup Water
- 3/4 Cup Milk

Directions:
1. Supply your smoker with wood pellets and follow the start-up procedure. Preheat the grill, with the lid closed, to 225° F. If using a gas or charcoal grill, set it up for low, indirect heat.
2. Peel, halve, and core apples.
3. Season apples with Tennessee Apple Butter then place directly on the grill grate, and smoke for 1 hour.
4. Meanwhile, prepare crêpe batter: combine eggs, milk, water, flour, and 3 tbsp of melted butter in a blender, and blend until smooth.
5. Refrigerate for 30 minutes.
6. Remove apples from grill, cool slightly, then slice thin.
7. Place a cast iron skillet on the grill and melt 3 tbsp butter with brown sugar, cinnamon, cornstarch, apple and lemon juices. Cook for 5 minutes until thick.
8. Add apples and cook for another 3 to 5 minutes, stirring to coat apples in sauce.
9. Remove from grill and set aside.
10. Preheat griddle to medium-low. If using a standard grill, preheat a cast iron skillet on medium-low heat.
11. Melt 1 teaspoon of butter on the griddle.
12. Then add ½ cup of batter, and spread with the bottom of a metal spatula, working quickly, as the batter cooks fast.
13. Cook one minute per side, until edges begin to brown. Remove from griddle, set aside, and repeat with remaining batter.
14. Spoon ¼ cup of apple filling into the center of each crêpe, then quarter-fold into a triangle.
15. Serve warm with additional apple filling, drizzle of warm caramel, and a dusting of cinnamon-sugar.

Mexican Black Bean Cornbread Casserole

Servings: 6
Cooking Time: 30 Minutes

Ingredients:
- 1 Lb Beef, Ground
- 1 15Oz Drained Black Beans, Can
- 1 Box Corn Muffin Mix
- 1 15Oz Enchilada Sauce, Can
- 1 Onion, Chopped
- 1 15Oz Drained Pinto Beans, Can

Directions:
1. Supply your smoker with wood pellets and follow the start-up procedure. Preheat the grill, with the lid closed, to 300° F.
2. Mix corn muffin mix according to directions.
3. Place cast iron skillet over flame broiler and heat for a few minutes, leaving Grill lid open.
4. Add onion and ground beef/sausage to skillet and break up
5. Cook until meat is done about 5 to 10 minutes.
6. Add both cans of beans, and enchilada sauce, stir to combine.
7. Bring mixture to a simmer.
8. Carefully close flame broiler and turn Grill up to 400 degrees.
9. Spread prepared corn muffin mix over top of meat and bean mixture and bake for 15 minutes until cornbread mixture is lightly browned.
10. Let sit 15 minutes before serving.

Marbled Brownies With Amaretto & Ricotta

Servings: 4
Cooking Time: 30 Minutes

Ingredients:
- 1 Cup Ricotta Cheese
- 1 eggs
- 1 Tablespoon Amaretto Liqueur
- 1/4 Cup sugar
- 2 Teaspoon cornstarch
- 1/2 Teaspoon vanilla extract
- 1 Brownie Mix

Directions:
1. Coat a 9- by 13-inch nonstick baking pan with cooking spray or softened butter and set aside. (If you do not have a nonstick pan, line a regular one with buttered foil or parchment paper.)
2. In a medium bowl, combine the ricotta, egg, amaretto, sugar, cornstarch, and vanilla and whisk together thoroughly. Set aside.
3. Prepare the brownie mix according to the package directions. Spread the brownie batter evenly in the prepared pan. Randomly drop dollops of the ricotta mixture over the batter. Run a plastic knife through the ricotta mixture to give the brownies a marbled look. (A plastic knife is less likely to scratch your pan's nonstick surface.)
4. Supply your smoker with wood pellets and follow the start-up procedure. Preheat the grill, with the lid closed, to 350° F.
5. Put the pan with the brownie mixture directly on the grill grate and bake, about 25 to 30 minutes. Insert a bamboo skewer or toothpick in the center of the brownies to determine if they are done: the batter should not be wet. Grill: 350 °F
6. Transfer the brownies to a wire cooling rack to cool completely. Cut into squares.

Savory Cheesecake With Bourbon Pecan Topping

Servings: 6
Cooking Time: 75 Minutes

Ingredients:
- Crust
- 12 ounce Oreos
- 6 ounce melted butter
- Filling
- 24 ounces cream cheese - room temperature
- 1 cup granulated sugar
- 3 tbs cornstarch
- 2 large eggs
- 2/3 cup heavy cream

- 1 tbs vanilla
- 1 1/2 tbs bourbon
- Topping
- 3 large eggs beaten
- 1/3 cup granulated sugar
- 1/3 cup brown sugar
- 8 tbsp corn syrup dark corn syrup recommended
- 2 tbsp bourbon
- 1/2 tbsp vanilla
- 1/8 tbsp salt
- 3/4 cup rough chopped pecans (smoked pecans recommended)

Directions:
1. Supply your smoker with wood pellets and follow the start-up procedure. Preheat the grill, with the lid closed, to 350 °F.
2. Wrap foil on the bottom and up the sides of a 9" spring-form pan (outside of pan).
3. Butter the bottom & insides of the pan.
4. Crust
5. Throw ingredients in a food processor until they are finely ground.
6. Spread in 9" cheesecake pan on bottom & about ½ way upsides.
7. Filling
8. Place 8 oz of cream cheese in mixer bowl with 1/3 of sugar & cornstarch. Mix until smooth andcreamy.
9. Add another 8 oz cream cheese andbeat until smooth, then add remaining cream cheese,beating until smooth.
10. Then mix in the rest of the sugar, bourbon & vanilla.
11. Add eggs one at a time beating well after each one.
12. Add the heavy cream and mix just until smooth. Reminder: Do not over mix.
13. Pour batter into the prepared crust.
14. Topping
15. Mix all together except pecans.
16. Sprinkle pecans on top of cheesecake batter.
17. Pour topping over cheesecake batter.
18. Place in a pan big enough to hold a spring-form pan. Pour boiling water in the roasting pan to come up about ½ way up the spring-form pan.
19. Bake at 350 °F for 75 minutes until the top just barely jiggles. Carefully take the pan out of water-bath and put on cooling rack.
20. Let cool for 2 hours in pan. After 2 hours put in fridge until totally chilled then serve.

Caramelized Bourbon Baked Pears

Servings: 4
Cooking Time: 30 Minutes

Ingredients:
- 3 Whole Pears, fresh
- 1/4 Cup brown sugar
- 1/4 Cup bourbon
- 2 Tablespoon butter, melted
- 1 Teaspoon vanilla extract
- 1/2 Teaspoon salt

Directions:
1. Supply your smoker with wood pellets and follow the start-up procedure. Preheat the grill, with the lid closed, to 325° F.
2. Peel and core the pears. Arrange them in a buttered baking dish.
3. In a small bowl, combine the brown sugar, bourbon, butter, vanilla, cinnamon and salt. Pour the bourbon mixture over the pears.

4. Place the baking dish on the grill grate, close the lid and bake for 30-35 minutes or until the pears are fork tender. Grill: 325 °F

5. Transfer to a serving plate and spoon the caramelized bourbon mixture over the pears.

6. Serve warm over vanilla ice cream. Enjoy!

Pumpkin Bread

Servings: 6
Cooking Time: 60 Minutes

Ingredients:
- 1 Cup Pumpkin, canned
- 2 eggs
- 2/3 Cup vegetable oil
- 1/2 Cup sour cream
- 1 Teaspoon vanilla extract
- 2 1/2 Cup flour
- 1 1/2 Teaspoon baking soda
- 1 Teaspoon salt
- 1/2 Teaspoon ground cinnamon
- 1/4 Teaspoon ground nutmeg
- 1/4 Teaspoon ground cloves
- 1/4 Teaspoon ground ginger
- As Needed butter

Directions:

1. In a large mixing bowl, combine the pumpkin, eggs, vegetable oil, sour cream, and vanilla and whisk to blend.

2. In a separate bowl, combine the flour, baking soda, salt, cinnamon, nutmeg, cloves, and ginger. Add the dry ingredients to the wet ingredients and stir to combine. Do not overmix.

3. If desired, stir in one or more of the optional ingredients (walnuts, dried cranberries, raisins, or chocolate chips). Butter the interiors of two loaf pans.

4. Sprinkle with flour to coat the buttered surfaces, and tap out any excess. Divide the batter evenly between the two pans.

5. When ready to cook, set the smoker to 350°F and preheat, lid closed for 15 minutes.

6. Arrange the loaf pans directly on the grill grate. Bake for 45 to 50 minutes, or until a skewer or toothpick inserted in the center comes out clean. Also, the top of the loaf should spring back when pressed gently with a finger.

7. Transfer the loaf pans to a cooling rack and let cool for 10 minutes before carefully turning out the pumpkin bread. Let the loaves cool thoroughly before slicing. Wrap in aluminum foil or plastic wrap if not eating right away. Serve and enjoy!

Bacon Chocolate Chip Cookies

Servings: 2
Cooking Time: 10-12 Minutes

Ingredients:
- 2¾ cups all-purpose flour
- 1½ teaspoons baking soda
- ½ teaspoon salt
- 12 tablespoons (1½ sticks) unsalted butter, softened
- 1 cup light brown sugar
- 1 cup granulated sugar
- 2 eggs, at room temperature
- 2½ teaspoons apple cider vinegar
- 1 teaspoon vanilla extract
- 2 cups semisweet chocolate chips
- 8 slices bacon, cooked and crumbled

Directions:

1. In a large bowl, combine the flour, baking soda, and salt, and mix well.

2. In a separate large bowl, using an electric mixer on medium speed, cream the butter and sugars. Reduce the speed to low and mix in the eggs, vinegar, and vanilla.
3. With the mixer speed still on low, slowly incorporate the dry ingredients, chocolate chips, and bacon pieces.
4. Supply your smoker with wood pellets and follow the start-up procedure. Preheat, with the lid closed, to 375°F.
5. Line a large baking sheet with parchment paper.
6. Drop rounded teaspoonfuls of cookie batter onto the prepared baking sheet and place on the grill grate. Close the lid and smoke for 10 to 12 minutes, or until the cookies are browned around the edges.

Delicious Pellet Grill Cornbread

Servings: 6
Cooking Time: 35 Minutes

Ingredients:

- 1 cup flour
- 1 cup cornmeal
- 2 teaspoons baking powder
- 2 teaspoons salt
- 3/4 cup sugar
- 2 tablespoons honey
- 1/2 cup butter
- 1 cup sour cream
- 3 eggs
- 1 cup milk

Directions:

1. Supply your smoker with wood pellets and follow the start-up procedure. Preheat the grill, with the lid closed, to 350° F.
2. Grease a 12-inch cast iron skillet or an equivalent baking pan.
3. Add flour, cornmeal, baking powder, salt, sugar, honey, butter, sour cream, eggs, and milk into a mixing bowl.
4. Mix well then pour into pan and bake on the grill for 30-35 minutes or until the cornbread is baked through in the center.

Ultimate Baked Garlic Bread

Servings: 4
Cooking Time: 20 Minutes

Ingredients:

- 1 baguette
- 1/2 Cup softened butter
- 1/2 Cup mayonnaise
- 4 Tablespoon chopped Italian parsley
- 6 Clove garlic, minced
- salt
- chile flakes
- 1 Cup mozzarella cheese
- 1/2 Cup Parmesan cheese

Directions:

1. Supply your smoker with wood pellets and follow the start-up procedure. Preheat the grill, with the lid closed, to 375° F.
2. Lay baguette on a cutting board and cut it in half lengthwise.
3. In a bowl, add butter, mayonnaise, parsley, garlic, salt and chile flakes. Mix well.
4. Spread butter mixture on baguette halves and top with mozzarella and Parmesan cheese.
5. Place baguette on the grill (if you like the bread crisp, do not use foil and if you like it soft, wrap with foil). Grill for approximately 15 to 25 minutes. Serve warm. Enjoy! Grill: 375 °F

Baked Bourbon Maple Pumpkin Pie

Servings: 6-8
Cooking Time: 60 Minutes

Ingredients:
- 1/4 Cup Cocoa Powder, Unsweetened
- 1 Tablespoon Cocoa Powder, Unsweetened
- 3 1/2 Tablespoon sugar
- 1 Teaspoon salt
- 1 1/4 Cup all-purpose flour
- 1 Tablespoon all-purpose flour
- 6 Tablespoon butter
- 2 Tablespoon vegetable oil
- 1 Large Egg Yolk
- 1/2 Teaspoon apple cider vinegar
- 1/4 Cup ice water
- 1 Large egg, beaten
- 15 Ounce Pumpkin, canned
- 1/4 Cup sour cream
- 2 Tablespoon bourbon
- 1 Teaspoon ground cinnamon
- 1/2 Teaspoon salt
- 1/4 Teaspoon ground ginger
- 1/4 Teaspoon ground nutmeg
- 1/8 Teaspoon Allspice, ground
- 1/8 Teaspoon Mace, ground
- 3 Large eggs
- 3/4 Cup maple syrup
- 2 Tablespoon sugar
- 1/2 Vanilla Bean, halved
- 1 Cup heavy cream

Directions:

1. For the Chocolate Pie Dough: Pulse cocoa powder, granulated sugar, salt, and 1-1/4 cups plus 1 Tbsp flour in a food processor to combine. Add butter and shortening and pulse until mixture resembles coarse meal with a few pea-sized pieces of butter remaining. Transfer to a large bowl.

2. Whisk together the egg yolk, vinegar, and 1/4 cup ice water in a small bowl. Drizzle half of the egg mixture over flour mixture and, using a fork, mix gently just until combined. Add remaining egg mixture and mix until the dough just comes together (you will have some unincorporated pieces).

3. Turn out dough onto a lightly floured surface, flatten slightly, and cut into quarters. Stack pieces on top of one another. Placing unincorporated dry pieces of dough between layers, and press down to combine. Repeat process twice more (all pieces of dough should be incorporated at this point). Form dough into a 1" thick disk. Wrap in plastic; chill at least 1 hour.

4. Roll out a disk of dough on a lightly floured surface into a 14" round. Transfer to a 9" pie dish. Lift up the edge and allow the dough to slump down into the dish. Trim. Leaving about 1" overhang. Fold overhang under and crimp edge. Chill in freezer 15 minutes.

5. When ready to cook, set the smoker to 350°F and preheat, lid closed for 15 minutes.

6. Line pie with parchment paper or heavy-duty foil, leaving a 1-1/2" overhang. Fill with pie weights or dried beans. Bake until crust is dry around the edge, about 20 minutes.

7. Remove paper and weights and bake until surface of the crust looks dry, 5-10 minutes.

8. Brush bottom and sides of crust with 1 beaten egg. Return to grill and bake until dry and set, about 3 minutes longer.

9. For the Pumpkin Maple Filling: Whisk together pumpkin puree, sour cream, bourbon,

cinnamon, salt, ginger, nutmeg, allspice, mace (optional) and remaining 3 eggs in a large bowl; set aside.

10. Pour maple syrup and 2 tbsp sugar in a small saucepan. Scrape in the seeds from vanilla bean (reserve pod for another use) or add vanilla extract and bring syrup to a boil. Reduce heat to medium-high and simmer, stirring occasionally, until mixture is thickened and small puffs of steam start to release about 3 minutes.

11. Remove from heat and add cream in 3 additions, stirring with a wooden spoon after each addition until smooth. Gradually whisk hot maple cream into pumpkin mixture.

12. Place pie dish on a rimmed baking sheet and pour in pumpkin filling. Bake pie, rotating halfway through, until set around edge but center barely jiggles 50-60 minutes.

13. Transfer pie dish to a wire rack and let the pie cool. Slice and serve. Enjoy!

Spiced Lemon Cherry Pie

Servings: 6-8
Cooking Time: 60 Minutes

Ingredients:
- 1/2 Teaspoon Cinnamon, Ground
- 1/2 Teaspoon Cloves, Ground
- 1/2 Cup Cornstarch
- 1 Pound Frozen Sweet Dark Cherries, Thawed
- 1 Teaspoon Water (Beaten With Egg) 1 Egg
- 1 Lemon, Juice
- 1 Lemon, Zest
- 2 Prepared Store Bought Or Homemade Pie Crust
- 1 Teaspoon Hickory Honey Sea Salt Seasoning
- 1 Cup Sugar, Granulated
- 1 Teaspoon Vanilla Extract

Directions:

1. In a large bowl, mix together the thawed cherries and their juices, sugar, cornstarch, lemon zest, lemon juice, cinnamon, clove, vanilla extract and Hickory Honey Sea Salt. Allow to sit for 30 minutes.

2. Flour a work surface and roll out one of the prepared pie crusts so that it fits a 9 inch pie tin. Fill with the cherry pie filling and refrigerate. When the pie is chilled, roll out the second pie crust, brush the edge of the first pie crust with the egg mixture, top with the second pie crust, crimp the edge with a fork, and chill. Alternatively, cut the second pie crust into strips and form a lattice pattern, attaching the strips with the egg mixture. Chill the pie for 15-30 minutes, or until the dough is very cold and firm. Brush the top of the pie with the remaining egg mixture.

3. Supply your smoker with wood pellets and follow the start-up procedure. Preheat the grill, with the lid closed, to 350° F and grill for 45 minutes to 1 hour, or until the pie crust is golden and firm and the filling is bubbly. Remove from the grill and allow to cool at room temperature for at least 4 hours to set the filling, then serve and enjoy!

Smoky Pimento Cheese Cornbread

Servings: 4
Cooking Time: 30 Minutes

Ingredients:
- 2 Tsp Baking Powder
- 2 Cups Buttermilk, Low Fat
- 1/2 Cup Cornmeal, Yellow

- 2 Egg
- 1 1/2 Cups Flour, All-Purpose
- 16 Oz Pimento Cheese Spread
- 2 Tbsp Bacon Cheddar Seasoning
- 1/4 Cup Sugar

Directions:
1. Supply your smoker with wood pellets and follow the start-up procedure. Preheat the grill, with the lid closed, to 350° F. Place a cast iron skillet in the grill to preheat.
2. In a bowl, mix together the eggs, buttermilk, Bacon Cheddar Seasoning, and pimento cheese spread. Add in the sugar, baking powder, cornmeal and flour. Mix until well combined.
3. With cooking gloves, carefully remove the cast iron skillet from the grill, grease it, and add the cornbread batter.
4. Grill for 25-30 minutes, or until the cornbread is golden and pulling away from the edges of the skillet.

Mint Butter Chocolate Chip Cookies

Servings: 24
Cooking Time: 12 Minutes

Ingredients:
- 1/2 Cup Butter, Melted
- 1 Package Chocolate Chip Cookie Mix
- 8-10 Drop Food Coloring
- 1/2 Tsp Mint, Extract

Directions:
1. Supply your smoker with wood pellets and follow the start-up procedure. Preheat the grill, with the lid closed, to 350° F.
2. Follow the directions on the back of the Chocolate Chip Cookie mix and also add the mint extract and green food coloring. Mix until combined.
3. On a baking sheet lined with parchment paper, drop balls of dough about 2 tbsp in size onto the pan.
4. Place in your Grill and bake for 10-12 minutes. Let cool for a couple minutes before removing from the pan. Enjoy!

Eggs Ham Benedict

Servings: 6
Cooking Time: 15 Minutes

Ingredients:
- 1 Biscuit Dough, Tube
- 6 Egg
- 16 Ham, Sliced
- 1 Packet Hollandaise Sauce, Package

Directions:
1. Supply your smoker with wood pellets and follow the start-up procedure. Preheat the grill, with the lid closed, to 350° F.
2. Grease a muffin tin and crack an egg in each cup. Place on the grate of the for about 10 minutes or until the whites are fully cooked.
3. At the same time, place your biscuit dough on a greased pan. Follow the directions on the packaging but bake on the . Place 2 slices of ham per biscuit on the pan as well.
4. While the ham, eggs, and biscuits are cooking, prepare the Hollandaise Sauce according to the directions on the packet.
5. When everything is fully cooked, cut a biscuit in half, and stack one or two slices of ham, 1 egg and a dollop of Hollandaise sauce. Repeat for each half biscuit. Serve with fresh fruit.

Skillet Buttermilk Cornbread

Servings: 6

Cooking Time: 25 Minutes

Ingredients:
- 1 Cup Cornmeal
- 1 Cup all-purpose flour
- 1/3 Cup granulated sugar
- 1 Teaspoon salt
- 1 Teaspoon baking powder
- 1 1/2 Cup buttermilk
- 2 Whole eggs
- 8 Tablespoon butter, melted

Directions:

1. Grease a cast iron skillet or 9-inch square baking pan with bacon fat. Put a 10-inch well-seasoned cast iron skillet on the grill grate. If using a regular baking pan, do not preheat.
2. Supply your smoker with wood pellets and follow the start-up procedure. Preheat the grill, with the lid closed, to 400° F.
3. In a large mixing bowl, combine the cornmeal, flour, sugar, salt, and baking powder and whisk to mix thoroughly. Make a well in the center of the dry ingredients.
4. In a separate mixing bowl, whisk together the buttermilk and eggs until well-combined. Add the melted butter. Pour into the dry ingredients and mix until the batter is fairly smooth. Do not overmix.
5. Carefully pour the batter into the preheated skillet. Bake for 20 to 25 minutes, or until the top is firm and a tester inserted in the center of the cornbread comes out clean. Be careful when removing the skillet from the grill as it will be very hot. Let the cornbread cool slightly on a trivet or cooling rack before slicing into wedges or squares.

Green Bean Casserole Circa 1955

Servings: 6

Cooking Time: 30 Minutes

Ingredients:
- 1 1/2 Pound Green Beans, fresh
- 1 Can cream of mushroom soup
- 1/2 Cup milk
- 2 Teaspoon soy sauce
- 1/2 Teaspoon Worcestershire sauce
- 1/2 Teaspoon black pepper
- 1.334 Cup French's Original Crispy Fried Onions
- 1/4 Cup red bell pepper, diced

Directions:

1. In a mixing bowl, combine the beans (trimmed and cooked until tender, or may use 2 16 oz. cans), soup, milk, soy sauce, Worcestershire sauce, black pepper, 2/3 cup of the onion rings, and red pepper, if using. Transfer to a 1-1/2 quart casserole dish.
2. Supply your smoker with wood pellets and follow the start-up procedure. Preheat the grill, with the lid closed, to 375° F.
3. Cook the casserole until the filling is hot and bubbling, 25 to 30 minutes. Top with the remaining onions and cook for 5 to 10 minutes more, or until the onions are crisp and beginning to brown. Grill: 375 °F

Baked Pumpkin Pie

Servings: 6

Cooking Time: 50 Minutes

Ingredients:
- 4 Ounce cream cheese
- 15 Ounce pumpkin puree
- 1/3 Cup Cream, whipping

- 1/2 Cup brown sugar
- 1 Teaspoon pumpkin pie spice
- 3 Large eggs
- 1 frozen pie crust, thawed

Directions:

1. Supply your smoker with wood pellets and follow the start-up procedure. Preheat the grill, with the lid closed, to 325° F.

2. Mix cream cheese, puree, milk, sugar, and spice. One at a time, incorporate an egg to the mixture. Pour mixture into pie shell.

3. Bake for 50 minutes, edges should be golden and pie should be firm around edges with slight movement in middle. Let cool before whip cream is applied. Serve and enjoy! Grill: 325 °F

Grilled Bourbon Pecan Pie

Servings: 6
Cooking Time: 45 Minutes

Ingredients:

- 2 Tbsp Bourbon
- 1/2 Cup Brown Sugar
- 1/3 Cup Unsalted Butter, Melted
- 1/2 Cup Light, 1/2 Cup Dark Corn Syrup
- 3 Egg
- 1/4 Tsp Hickory Honey Smoked Salt
- Decoration Pecan
- 1 1/4 Cup Chopped Pecans, Coarsely Broken
- 1 Prepared Or Homemade Pie Shell, Deep
- 1/2 Cup Sugar
- 1 Tsp Vanilla Extract

Directions:

1. Supply your smoker with wood pellets and follow the start-up procedure. Preheat the grill, with the lid closed, to 375° F. Meanwhile, prepare your pie crust in a 9 cast iron skillet or heat proof pie plate.

2. In a large bowl, beat the eggs until smooth. Add the brown sugar and white sugar and mix until smooth. Add the light corn syrup, dark corn syrup, vanilla, bourbon, melted butter, and Hickory Honey Salt. Mix until smooth. Stir in your chopped pecans and pour into the pie crust. Top with the whole pecans, if desired.

3. Grill covered for 35-45 minutes, until the pie is just set around the edges but still has a slight jiggle in the center.

4. Allow the pie to cool completely before slicing. Enjoy!

Smoked Blackberry Pie

Servings: 4-6
Cooking Time: 25 Minutes

Ingredients:

- Nonstick cooking spray or butter, for greasing
- 1 box (2 sheets) refrigerated piecrusts
- 8 tablespoons (1 stick) unsalted butter, melted, plus 8 tablespoons (1 stick) cut into pieces
- ½ cup all-purpose flour
- 2 cups sugar, divided
- 2 pints blackberries
- ½ cup milk
- Vanilla ice cream, for serving

Directions:

1. Supply your smoker with wood pellets and follow the start-up procedure. Preheat, with the lid closed, to 375°F.

2. Coat a cast iron skillet with cooking spray.

3. Unroll 1 refrigerated piecrust and place in the bottom and up the side of the skillet. Using a fork poke holes in the crust in several places.

4. Set the skillet on the grill grate, close the lid, and smoke for 5 minutes, or until lightly browned Remove from the grill and set aside.

5. In a large bowl, combine the stick of melted butter with the flour and 1½ cups of sugar.
6. Add the blackberries to the flour-sugar mixture and toss until well coated.
7. Spread the berry mixture evenly in the skillet and sprinkle the milk on top. Scatter half of the cut pieces of butter randomly over the mixture.
8. Unroll the remaining piecrust and place it over the top of skillet or slice the dough into even strips and weave it into a lattice. Scatter the remaining pieces of butter along the top of the crust.
9. Sprinkle the remaining ½ cup of sugar on top of the crust and return the skillet to the smoker.
10. Close the lid and smoke for 15 to 20 minutes, or until bubbly and brown on top. It may be necessary to use some aluminum foil around the edges near the end of the cooking time to prevent the crust from burning.
11. Serve the pie hot with vanilla ice cream.

Sweet And Spicy Baked Pork Beans

Servings: 20
Cooking Time: 120 Minutes

Ingredients:
- 1 - 21 Oz Apple Pie Filling, Can
- 1 Gallon Baked Beans
- 1 Tbs Chilli, Powder
- 1 Green Bell Pepper, Diced
- 1 10 Oz Drained Jalapeno, Can Diced
- 1 Cup Maple Syrup
- 1 Onion, Diced
- 1 Lb Pork, Pulled

Directions:
1. Supply your smoker with wood pellets and follow the start-up procedure. Preheat the grill, with the lid closed, to 350° F.
2. Place all ingredients in mixing bowl and mix well.
3. Pour bean mixture into foil pans.
4. Bake in grill till bubbling throughout – about 2 hours.
5. Rest at least 15 minutes before serving.

Dark Chocolate Brownies With Bacon-salted Caramel

Servings: 8
Cooking Time: 40 Minutes

Ingredients:
- 8 Strips bacon
- 1/2 Cup kosher salt
- 1 Whole Brownie Mix
- 1 Jar caramel sauce

Directions:
1. For the bacon salt: Cook a few strips of bacon (6 to 8) until very crisp: 350 degrees for about 25 minutes should do it. Let cool, then pulse in a food processor until finely chopped. Mix with 1/2 cup kosher salt. Store in the refrigerator until ready to use.
2. Supply your smoker with wood pellets and follow the start-up procedure. Preheat the grill, with the lid closed, to 350° F.
3. Mix the brownies according to package directions and pour into a greased pan. Drizzle approximately 2 tablespoons of the caramel sauce over the brownie batter. Sprinkle with approximately 1 teaspoon of the bacon salt. Place directly on the grill grate of your preheated Traeger.

4. Bake the brownies for 20-25 minutes, until the batter has started to set up. Remove from the grill and drizzle with 2 more tablespoons of caramel sauce and sprinkle with more bacon salt. Return to the grill for 20-25 more minutes, or until a toothpick inserted in the middle of the brownies comes out clean.

5. If you like extra caramel, drizzle another layer of caramel on the hot brownies and sprinkle with a final bit of bacon salt. Allow the brownies to cool completely before cutting them into squares. Clean your knife in between each slice to prevent the brownies from sticking to the knife. Enjoy!

Chocolate Lava Cake With Smoked Whipped Cream

Servings: 4
Cooking Time: 45 Minutes

Ingredients:
- 1 Pint heavy whipping cream
- 9 Tablespoon Butter
- 220 G Semisweet Chocolate
- 1 1/4 Cup powdered sugar
- 2 Large eggs
- 2 egg yolk
- 6 Tablespoon flour
- 1 Tablespoon Bourbon Vanilla
- Powdered Sugar
- cocoa powder

Directions:

1. Supply your smoker with wood pellets and follow the start-up procedure. Preheat the grill, with the lid closed, to 180° F.

2. For the Smoked Whipped Cream: Add cream to a shallow, aluminum baking pan. Place the pan on the grill and smoke for 30 minutes.

3. Pour the smoked cream into a large mixing bowl and refrigerate for later use. Grill: 180 °F

4. Increase the grill temperature to 375°F and preheat. Grill: 375 °F

5. Brush 4 small soufflé cups with 1 tablespoon melted butter.

6. Melt the chocolate and remaining butter in a heatproof bowl over simmering water, stir until smooth.

7. Stir in powdered sugar. Add eggs and egg yolks, stirring continuously. Whisk in flour until blended completely.

8. Pour batter into the prepared soufflé cups. Place them on the Traeger and bake for 13-14 minutes, or until the sides are set. Grill: 375 °F

9. For the Whipped Cream: Remove the chilled smoked cream from the refrigerator, add the bourbon vanilla and whip until airy.

10. Add confectioners sugar and continue whipping until whipped cream forms stiff peaks.

11. Dust lava cakes with confectioners sugar and cocoa, top with a dollop of smoke-infused whipped cream. Enjoy!

Sourdough Pizza

Servings: 4
Cooking Time: 12 Minutes

Ingredients:
- 1 1/2 Cup Fresh Sourdough Starter
- 1 Tablespoon olive oil
- 1 Teaspoon Jacobsen Salt Co. Pure Kosher Sea Salt
- 1 1/4 Cup all-purpose flour

Directions:

1. Supply your smoker with wood pellets and follow the start-up procedure. Preheat the grill, with the lid closed, to 450° F.

2. Mix together the fresh sourdough starter, one tablespoon of oil, Jacobsen salt and 1-1/4 cups of flour. Add more flour, a little at a time, as needed to form a pizza dough consistency.

3. Allow the dough to rest for 30 minutes, to allow for easier rolling. Roll the dough out into a circle, using a small amount of flour to prevent sticking.

4. Place on a pizza stone. Bake the crust for approximately 7 minutes Grill: 450 °F

5. Remove the crust from the grill; brush on remaining oil to prevent toppings from soaking into the crust. Add the desired toppings and return pizza to grill; bake until the crust browns and the cheese melts.

Rosemary Cranberry Apple Sage Stuffing

Servings: 7
Cooking Time: 45 Minutes

Ingredients:
- 10 Cups Day Old Diced Bread, Sliced Loaf
- 2 1/2 Cups Broth, Chicken
- 1 Cup Butter, Unsalted
- 1 Cup Diced Celery, Cut
- 1 1/2 Cups Fresh Cranberries
- 1 Beaten Egg
- 1 Medium Granny Smith Apple, Peel, Core And Dice
- 2 Tbsp Minced Parsley, Fresh
- 1 Tbsp Minced Rosemary, Fresh
- 2 Tbsp Roughly Chopped Sage
- Salt And Pepper
- 1 Tbsp Minced Thyme
- 2 Cups Diced Yellow Onion, Sliced

Directions:

1. Supply your smoker with wood pellets and follow the start-up procedure. Preheat the grill, with the lid closed, to 350° F.

2. Melt butter over medium heat. Add onions then celery and cook until onions start to become translucent.

3. In a large bowl, mix together bread, apples, cranberries, cooked onion and celery mixture, and fresh herbs.

4. Add half of the chicken broth to the mixture and stir.

5. Beat together eggs and the rest of the chicken broth in a small bowl. Pour into the bread mixture and stir until completely combined.

6. Add salt and pepper to taste.

7. Pour stuffing into a cast iron pan or baking dish. Cover with foil and bake on the grill for 30 minutes. Remove the foil and cook for an additional 15 minutes.

8. Serve immediately and enjoy!

Pull-apart Dinner Rolls

Servings: 8
Cooking Time: 10 Minutes

Ingredients:
- 1/4 Cup warm water (110°F to 115°F)
- 1/3 Cup vegetable oil
- 2 Tablespoon active dry yeast
- 1/4 Cup sugar
- 1/2 Teaspoon salt
- 1 egg
- 3 1/2 Cup all-purpose flour
- cooking spray

Directions:

1. Supply your smoker with wood pellets and follow the start-up procedure. Preheat the grill, with the lid closed, to 400° F.

2. In the bowl of a stand mixer, combine warm water, oil, yeast and sugar. Let mixture rest for 5 to 10 minutes, or until frothy and bubbly.
3. With a dough hook, mix in salt, egg and 2 cups of flour until combined. Add remaining flour 1/2 cup at a time (dough will be sticky).
4. Prepare a cast iron pan with cooking spray and set aside.
5. Spray your hands with cooking spray and shape the dough into 12 balls.
6. After shaped, place in the prepared cast iron pan and let rest for 10 minutes. Bake in Traeger for about 10 to 12 minutes, or until tops are lightly golden. Enjoy! Grill: 400 °F

Donut Bread Pudding

Servings: 8
Cooking Time: 40 Minutes

Ingredients:
- 16 Cake Donuts
- 1/2 Cup Raisins, seedless
- 5 eggs
- 3/4 Cup sugar
- 2 Cup heavy cream
- 2 Teaspoon vanilla extract
- 1 Teaspoon ground cinnamon
- 3/4 Cup Butter, melted, cooled slightly
- Ice Cream

Directions:
1. Lightly butter a 9- by 13-inch baking pan. Layer the donuts in an even thickness in the pan. Distribute the raisins over the top, if using. Drizzle evenly with the butter.
2. Make the custard: In a medium bowl, whisk together the sugar, eggs, cream, vanilla, and cinnamon. Whisk in the butter. Pour over the donuts. Let sit for 10 to 15 minutes, periodically pushing the donuts down into the custard. Cover with foil.
3. Supply your smoker with wood pellets and follow the start-up procedure. Preheat the grill, with the lid closed, to 350° F.
4. Bake the bread pudding for 30 to 40 minutes, or until the custard is set. Remove the foil and continue to bake for 10 additional minutes to lightly brown the top. Grill: 350 °F
5. Let cool slightly before cutting into squares. Drizzle with melted ice cream, if desired. Enjoy!

SEAFOOD RECIPES

Smoked Honey Salmon

Servings: 2
Cooking Time: 25 Minutes

Ingredients:
- 1 lb. salmon fillets
- 1/2 tsp. pepper
- 1/4 tsp. salt
- 2 tbsp. sriracha
- 2 tsp. honey
- 2 tsp. chili sauce
- 1 tsp. lime juice
- 1/2 tsp. fish sauce

Directions:
1. Supply your smoker with wood pellets and follow the start-up procedure. Preheat the grill, with the lid closed, to 350° F.
2. Sprinkle the salmon with salt and pepper.
3. In a bowl, whisk together the sriracha, honey, chili sauce, lime juice, and fish sauce.
4. Once the grill is hot, place the salmon on the grill and leave for 15 minutes.
5. After 15 minutes, brush the salmon with the sriracha chili sauce and keep cooking for 5-10minutes. The salmon should be firm to the touch and crispy on the edges.
6. Serve hot!

Delicious Smoked Trout

Servings: 8
Cooking Time: 120 Minutes

Ingredients:
- 6 rainbow trout fillets
- Brine:
- 2 Tablespoons kosher salt
- 2 Tablespoons brown sugar
- 4 cups cool water

Directions:
1. For the brine, dissolve the kosher salt and brown sugar in water.
2. Place the trout fillets in the brine, skin side up, and brine the fillets for 15 minutes.
3. Supply your smoker with wood pellets and follow the start-up procedure. Preheat the grill, with the lid closed, to 180° F.
4. Remove the trout from the brine and transfer it to the grill grates.
5. Smoke the trout for 1.5 to 2 hours with the lid closed, depending on the thickness of your fillets.
6. Smoke until the trout reaches an internal temperature of 145 °F, or until the trout flakes easily.
7. Remove the trout from the smoker and serve warm, or let it cool completely and serve chilled with your favorite accouterments.

Garlic Pepper Shrimp Pesto Bruschetta

Servings: 12
Cooking Time: 15 Minutes

Ingredients:
- 12 Slices Bread, Baguette
- 1/2 Tsp Chili Pepper Flakes
- 1/2 Tsp Garlic Powder
- 4 Cloves Garlic, Minced
- 2 Tbsp Olive Oil
- 1/2 Tsp Paprika, Smoked

- 1/4 Tsp Parsley, Leaves
- Pepper
- Pesto
- Salt
- 12 Shrimp, Jumbo

Directions:

1. Supply your smoker with wood pellets and follow the start-up procedure. Preheat the grill, with the lid closed, to 350° F. Place the baguette slices on a baking sheet lined with foil. Stir together the olive oil, and minced garlic, then brush both sides of the baguette slices with the mix. Place the pan inside the grill, and bake for about 10-15 minutes.

2. In a skillet, add a splash of olive oil, shrimp, chili powder, garlic powder, smoked paprika, salt pepper, and grill on medium-high heat for about 5 minutes (until the shrimp is pink). Be sure to stir often. Once pink, remove pan from heat. Once the baguettes are toasted, let them cool for 5 minutes, then spread a layer of pesto onto each one, then top with a shrimp, and serve.

Traeger Smoked Salmon

Servings: 6
Cooking Time: 240 Minutes

Ingredients:

- 1 (2-1/2 to 3 lb) salmon fillet
- 1/2 Cup kosher salt
- 1 Cup brown sugar, firmly packed
- 1 Tablespoon ground black pepper

Directions:

1. Remove all pin bones from salmon.
2. In a small bowl, combine salt, sugar and black pepper. Lay a large piece of plastic wrap on a flat surface that is at least 6 inches longer than the fillet. Spread 1/2 of the mixture on top of the plastic and lay the fillet skin side down on top of the cure. Top with the other 1/2 of the cure spreading it evenly over the top of the fillet. Fold up the edges of the plastic and wrap tightly.

3. Place the wrapped salmon fillet in the bottom of a flat, rectangle baking dish or hotel pan. Place another identical pan on top of the fillet. Place a couple of cans or something heavy inside the top pan to weigh it down making sure the weight is distributed evenly.

4. Transfer the weighted salmon to the refrigerator and cure for 4 to 6 hours.

5. Remove the salmon from the plastic wrap and rinse the cure thoroughly (not rinsing thoroughly will result in a salty finished product). Place skin side down on a wire rack atop a sheet tray and pat dry. Place the sheet tray in the refrigerator and allow the salmon to dry overnight. This allows a tacky film called a pellicle to form on the surface of the salmon. The pellicle helps smoke adhere to the fish.

6. Supply your smoker with wood pellets and follow the start-up procedure. Preheat the grill, with the lid closed, to 180° F.

7. Place the salmon skin side down directly on the grill grate and smoke for 3 to 4 hours or until the internal temperature of the fish registers 140°F. Enjoy warm or chilled. Grill: 180 °F Probe: 140 °F

Barbecued Shrimp

Servings: 4
Cooking Time: 10 Minutes

Ingredients:

- 1 pound peeled and deveined shrimp, with tails on
- 2 tablespoons olive oil

- 1 batch Dill Seafood Rub

Directions:
1. Soak wooden skewers in water for 30 minutes.
2. Supply your smoker with wood pellets and follow the start-up procedure. Preheat the grill, with the lid closed, to 375°F.
3. Thread 4 or 5 shrimp per skewer.
4. Coat the shrimp all over with olive oil and season each side of the skewers with the rub.
5. Place the skewers directly on the grill grate and grill the shrimp for 5 minutes per side. Remove the skewers from the grill and serve immediately.

Teriyaki Smoked Honey Tilapia

Servings: 4
Cooking Time: 120 Minutes

Ingredients:
- 4 tilapia fillets
- 1 cup teriyaki sauce
- 2/3 cup honey
- 1 tbsp sriracha sauce
- Green onions (optional)

Directions:
1. In a large bowl, make the marinade by mixing together the teriyaki sauce, honey, and sriracha. Make sure honey is dissolved and well blended.
2. Place the tilapia fillets in the marinade. Turn the fillets so they are completely coated. Cover with a plastic wrap and marinate in the fridge for about 2 hours.
3. Supply your smoker with wood pellets and follow the start-up procedure. Preheat the grill, with the lid closed, to 275° F.
4. Remove the tilapia fillets from the marinade and transfer them to the grill. Smoke the fillets until they reach an internal temperature of 145°F, about 2 hours.
5. Sprinkle with green onions if desired.

Smoked Cedar Plank Salmon

Servings: 4
Cooking Time: 20 Minutes

Ingredients:
- 1/4 Cup Brown Sugar
- 1/2 Tablespoon Olive Oil
- Competition Smoked Seasoning
- 4 Salmon Fillets, Skin Off

Directions:
1. Soak the untreated cedar plank in water for 24 hours before grilling. When ready to grill, remove and wipe down.
2. Supply your smoker with wood pellets and follow the start-up procedure. Preheat the grill, with the lid closed, to 350° F.
3. In a small bowl, mix the brown sugar, oil, and Lemon Pepper, Garlic, and Herb seasoning. Rub generously over the salmon fillets.
4. Place the plank over indirect heat, then lay the salmon on the plank and grill for 15-20 minutes, or until the salmon is cooked through and flakes easily with a fork. Remove from the heat and serve immediately.

Cedar Smoked Garlic Salmon

Servings: 6
Cooking Time: 60 Minutes

Ingredients:
- 1 Tsp Black Pepper
- 3 Cedar Plank, Untreated
- 1 Tsp Garlic, Minced
- 1/3 Cup Olive Oil
- 1 Tsp Onion, Salt

- 1 Tsp Parsley, Minced Fresh
- 1 1/2 Tbsp Rice Vinegar
- 2 Salmon, Fillets (Skin Removed)
- 1 Tsp Sesame Oil
- 1/3 Cup Soy Sauce

Directions:

1. Soak the cedar planks in warm water for an hour or more.
2. In a bowl, mix together the olive oil, rice vinegar, sesame oil, soy sauce, and minced garlic.
3. Add in the salmon and let it marinate for about 30 minutes.
4. Start your grill on smoke with the lid open until a fire is established in the burn pot (3-7 minutes).
5. Supply your smoker with wood pellets and follow the start-up procedure. Preheat the grill, with the lid closed, to 225° F.
6. Place the planks on the grate. Once the boards start to smoke and crackle a little, it's ready for the fish.
7. Remove the fish from the marinade, season it with the onion powder, parsley and black pepper, then discard the marinade.
8. Place the salmon on the planks and grill until it reaches 140°F internal temperature (start checking temp after the salmon has been on the grill for 30 minutes).
9. Remove from the grill, let it rest for 10 minutes, then serve.

Garlic Bacon Wrapped Shrimp

Servings: 4
Cooking Time: 11 Minutes

Ingredients:

- 8 Bacon, Strip
- 1/4 Cup Butter Style Shortening (Melted)
- 1 Clove Garlic, Minced
- 1 Tsp Lemon, Juice
- Pepper
- Salt
- 16 (Peeled And Veined) Shrimp, Jumbo

Directions:

1. Supply your smoker with wood pellets and follow the start-up procedure. Preheat the grill, with the lid closed, to 450° F.
2. Take one slice of bacon, and wrap it around each piece of shrimp, and lock it in place with a wooden toothpick.
3. Place the shortening into a mixing bowl and whisk in the garlic and lemon juice. Brush each shrimp with the sauce on both sides.
4. Place on the grill, and barbecue for 11 minutes.
5. Turn the grill off, remove the shrimp, serve and enjoy!

Coconut Shrimp Jalapeño Poppers

Servings: 6
Cooking Time: 55 Minutes

Ingredients:

- 8 Whole shrimp, peeled and deveined
- 1/2 Teaspoon Chicken Rub, plus more as needed
- olive oil
- 6 Whole jalapeños
- 8 Ounce cream cheese, softened
- 2 Tablespoon fresh chopped cilantro
- 1/2 Cup unsweetened coconut flakes
- 12 Slices bacon

Directions:

1. Supply your smoker with wood pellets and follow the start-up procedure. Preheat the grill, with the lid closed, to 425° F.
2. Rinse and season the shrimp with the Traeger Chicken Rub.
3. Drizzle the shrimp with olive oil and cook on the Traeger for about 5 minutes per side, or until the shrimp is opaque. Grill: 425 °F
4. Remove the shrimp and let cool.
5. Reduce Traeger temperature to 350°F. Grill: 350 °F
6. Meanwhile, get those poppers going. Cut the jalapeños in half then remove the stems and seeds.
7. Chop the shrimp. Mix together the softened cream cheese, chopped shrimp, 1/2 teaspoon Traeger Chicken Rub and 2 tablespoons chopped cilantro.
8. Load a generous amount of the filling in each pepper half. Top with a sprinkle of coconut.
9. Wrap each stuffed pepper with a slice of bacon and place on a foil-lined baking sheet.
10. Cook the peppers on the Traeger for about 45 minutes, or until the bacon fat has rendered and the cream cheese is golden. Enjoy! Grill: 350 °F

Charleston Crab Cakes With Remoulade

Servings: 4
Cooking Time: 45 Minutes

Ingredients:
- 1¼ cups mayonnaise
- ¼ cup yellow mustard
- 2 tablespoons sweet pickle relish, with its juices
- 1 tablespoon smoked paprika
- 2 teaspoons Cajun seasoning
- 2 teaspoons prepared horseradish
- 1 teaspoon hot sauce
- 1 garlic clove, finely minced
- 2 pounds fresh lump crabmeat, picked clean
- 20 butter crackers (such as Ritz brand), crushed
- 2 tablespoons Dijon mustard
- 1 cup mayonnaise
- 2 tablespoons freshly squeezed lemon juice
- 1 tablespoon salted butter, melted
- 1 tablespoon Worcestershire sauce
- 1 tablespoon Old Bay seasoning
- 2 teaspoons chopped fresh parsley
- 1 teaspoon ground mustard
- 2 eggs, beaten
- ¼ cup extra-virgin olive oil, divided

Directions:
1. For the remoulade:
2. In a small bowl, combine the mayonnaise, mustard, pickle relish, paprika, Cajun seasoning, horseradish, hot sauce, and garlic.
3. Refrigerate until ready to serve.
4. For the crab cakes:
5. Supply your smoker with wood pellets and follow the start-up procedure. Preheat, with the lid closed, to 375°F.
6. Spread the crabmeat on a foil-lined baking sheet and place over indirect heat on the grill, with the lid closed, for 30 minutes.
7. Remove from the heat and let cool for 15 minutes.
8. While the crab cools, combine the crushed crackers, Dijon mustard, mayonnaise, lemon juice, melted butter, Worcestershire sauce, Old Bay, parsley, ground mustard, and eggs until well incorporated.
9. Fold in the smoked crabmeat, then shape the mixture into 8 (1-inch-thick) crab cakes.

10. In a large skillet or cast-iron pan on the grill, heat 2 tablespoons of olive oil. Add half of the crab cakes, close the lid, and smoke for 4 to 5 minutes on each side, or until crispy and golden brown.

11. Remove the crab cakes from the pan and transfer to a wire rack to drain. Pat them to remove any excess oil.

12. Repeat steps 6 and 7 with the remaining oil and crab cakes.

13. Serve the crab cakes with the remoulade.

Grilled Lemon Lobster Tails

Servings: 3
Cooking Time: 7 Minutes

Ingredients:
- 6 lobster tails
- 1/4 cup melted butter
- 1/4 cup fresh lemon juice
- 1 tablespoon fresh dill
- 1 teaspoon salt
- 6 lime wedges

Directions:
1. Supply your smoker with wood pellets and follow the start-up procedure. Preheat the grill, with the lid closed, to 375° F.
2. Split the lobster tails in half place then back side down.
3. Cut down through the center to the shell the whole length of each tail.
4. Pull the shell back, exposing the meat.
5. Pat the lobster tails with paper towel to dry.
6. Combine in a small mixing bowl the butter, lemon juice, dill, and salt until the salt has dissolved.
7. Brush the mixture onto the flesh side of each lobster tail.
8. Place the lobster tails onto the grill and cook for 5 to 7 minutes, turning them once during the cooking process. (The shells should turn a bright pink).
9. Remove the heat.
10. Serve with lime wedges!

Grilled Whole Steelhead Fillet

Servings: 6
Cooking Time: 30 Minutes

Ingredients:
- (2-1/2 to 3 lb) steelhead or salmon fillet, skin-on
- 2 Tablespoon Montana Mex Sweet Seasoning
- 1 Teaspoon Montana Mex Jalapeño Seasoning Blend
- 1 Teaspoon Montana Mex Mild Chile Seasoning Blend
- 2 Tablespoon Montana Mex Avocado Oil
- 2 Tablespoon freshly grated ginger
- 1 lemon, thinly sliced

Directions:
1. Coat fillet evenly with all three dry seasonings avocado oil, grated ginger and thinly sliced lemon.
2. Supply your smoker with wood pellets and follow the start-up procedure. Preheat the grill, with the lid closed, to 380° F.
3. Place the fish skin-side down on the grill grate and cook for 20 minutes. Grill: 380 °F
4. Remove fillet from grill and let rest for 5 minutes. Enjoy!

Smoke-roasted Halibut With Mixed Herb Vinaigrette

Servings: 4
Cooking Time: 12 Minutes

Ingredients:
- 4 halibut fillets, each about 6 to 8oz (170 to 225g)
- for the vinaigrette
- 2 tbsp white wine vinegar or sherry vinegar, plus more
- ¼ tsp coarse salt, plus more
- ¼ tsp freshly ground black pepper, plus more
- ½ cup extra virgin olive oil
- 2 tbsp minced fresh herbs, such as dill, flat-leaf parsley, or oregano
- for serving
- 4 cups loosely packed baby arugula, spinach, or other mixed greens
- 1 lemon, cut lengthwise into 4 wedges

Directions:
1. Supply your smoker with wood pellets and follow the start-up procedure. Preheat the grill, with the lid closed, to 400° F.
2. In a small bowl, make the vinaigrette by whisking together the vinegar, and salt and pepper. Whisk until the salt dissolves. Continue to whisk while slowly adding the olive oil. Whisk until the vinaigrette is emulsified. Stir in the herbs. Taste, adding vinegar or salt and pepper to taste. Pour 1/3 of the vinaigrette into a separate container. Reserve the remainder.
3. Place the fillets on a rimmed sheet pan. Lightly brush both sides with the smaller portion of vinaigrette. (Dividing the vinaigrette into two containers prevents cross-contamination.) Lightly season with salt and pepper.
4. Place the fillets on the grate at an angle to the bars. Grill until the edges begin to look opaque, about 4 to 6 minutes. Gently turn and grill until the fish is cooked through, about 4 to 6 minutes more. (A fillet will break into clean flakes when pressed with a fork when it's done.)
5. Remove the fish from the grill. Place the greens in a large bowl and toss them with 2 to 3 tablespoons of the reserved vinaigrette (you want the greens lightly coated) and divide between 4 plates. Place a fillet on the greens on each plate. Drizzle a bit more of the vinaigrette over the top. Serve with lemon wedges.

Spicy Lime Shrimp

Servings: 4
Cooking Time: 10 Minutes

Ingredients:
- 2 Tsp Chili Paste
- 1/2 Tsp Cumin
- 2 Cloves Garlic, Minced
- 1 Large Lime, Juiced
- 1/4 Tsp Paprika, Powder
- 1/4 Tsp Red Flakes Pepper
- 1/2 Tsp Salt

Directions:
1. In a bowl, whisk together the lime juice, olive oil, garlic, chili powder, cumin, paprika, salt, pepper, and red pepper flakes.
2. Then pour it into a resealable bag, add the shrimp, toss the coat, let it marinate for 30 minutes.
3. Supply your smoker with wood pellets and follow the start-up procedure. Preheat the grill, with the lid closed, to 400° F.
4. Next place the shrimp on skewers, place on the grill, and grill each side for about two minutes until it's done. One finished, remove the shrimp from the grill and enjoy!

Grilled Lobster Tails With Smoked Paprika Butter

Servings: 4
Cooking Time: 10-12 Minutes

Ingredients:
- 4 lobster tails, each about 8 to 10oz (225 to 285g), thawed if frozen
- 3 lemons, 1 quartered lengthwise, 2 halved through their equators
- for the butter
- 1¼ cup unsalted butter, at room temperature
- 2 garlic cloves, peeled and finely minced
- 3 tbsp chopped fresh parsley
- 2 tbsp chopped fresh chives
- 1 tbsp freshly squeezed lemon juice
- 2 tsp finely chopped lemon zest
- 2 tsp smoked paprika
- 1 tsp coarse salt

Directions:
1. Supply your smoker with wood pellets and follow the start-up procedure. Preheat the grill, with the lid closed, to 450° F.
2. In a medium bowl, make the paprika butter by combining the ingredients. Beat with a wooden spoon until well blended.
3. Use a sharp, heavy knife or sturdy kitchen shears to cut lengthwise through the top shell of each lobster tail in a straight line toward the tail fin. Gently loosen the meat from the bottom shell and sides. Lift the meat through the slit you just made so the meat sits on top of the shell. Slip a lemon quarter underneath the meat (between the meat and the bottom shell) to keep it elevated. Spread 1 tablespoon of paprika butter on top of each lobster. Melt the remaining butter and keep it warm.
4. Place the lobster tails flesh side up and lemon halves cut sides down on the grate. Grill the lobsters until the flesh is white and opaque and the internal temperature of the lobster meat reaches 135 to 140°F (57 to 60°C), about 10 to 12 minutes, basting at least once with some of the melted butter. (Don't overcook or the lobster will become unpleasantly rubbery.)
5. Transfer the lobsters and the lemon halves to a platter. Divide the remaining melted butter between 4 ramekins before serving.

Salmon Cakes With Homemade Tartar Sauce

Servings: 4
Cooking Time: 15 Minutes

Ingredients:
- 1 1/2 Cups Breadcrumb, Dry
- 1/2 Tablespoon Capers, Diced
- 1/4 Cup Dill Pickle Relish
- 2 Eggs
- 1 1/4 Cup Mayonnaise, Divided
- 1 Tablespoon Mustard, Grainy
- 1/2 Tablespoon Olive Oil
- 1/2 Red Pepper, Diced Finely
- 1/2 Tablespoon Sweet Rib Rub
- 1 Cup Cooked Salmon, Flaked

Directions:
1. In a large bowl, mix together the salmon, eggs, ¼ cup mayonnaise, breadcrumbs, red bell pepper, Sweet Rib Rub, and mustard. Allow the mixture to sit for 15 minutes to hydrate the breadcrumbs.
2. Supply your smoker with wood pellets and follow the start-up procedure. Preheat the grill, with the lid closed, to 350° F.

3. In a small bowl, mix together the remaining mayonnaise, dill pickle relish, and diced capers. Set aside.

4. Place the baking sheet on the grill to preheat. Once the baking sheet is hot, drizzle the olive oil over the pan and drop rounded tablespoons of the salmon mixture onto the sheet pan. Press the mixture down into a flat patty with a spatula. Allow to grill for 3 to 5 minutes, then flip and grill for 1 to 2 more minutes. Remove from the grill and serve with the reserved tartar sauce.

Grilled Albacore Tuna With Potato-tomato Casserole

Servings: 8
Cooking Time: 20 Minutes

Ingredients:
- 6 Tuna Steaks, 6oz
- 1 Whole lemon zest
- 1 chile de árbol, thinly sliced
- 1 Tablespoon thyme
- 1 Tablespoon fresh parsley

Directions:
1. To make the fish: Season the fish with the lemon zest, chile, thyme, and parsley. Cover and refrigerate at least 4 hours.
2. Remove fish from the refrigerator 30 minutes before cooking to come to room temperature.
3. Season the fish with salt and pepper on both sides. Grill 2-3 minutes per side (next to the cast iron with the casserole) rotating it once or twice. The tuna should be well seared but still rare.

Baked Whole Fish In Sea Salt

Servings: 4
Cooking Time: 30 Minutes

Ingredients:
- 3 Pound Whole Branzino, (1.5 each)
- 10 Sprig thyme sprigs
- 1 Medium lemon, thinly sliced
- 5 Cup sea salt
- 10 Whole egg white
- olive oil
- 1 Whole lemon juice

Directions:
1. Supply your smoker with wood pellets and follow the start-up procedure. Preheat the grill, with the lid closed, to High heat.
2. Clip the fins and remove the gills from the fish. Stuff cavity with thyme and lemon slices. Whip the egg whites to soft peaks and fold in the sea salt.
3. Place directly on the grill grate and bake for 30 minutes or until a thermometer poked through the salt crust and into the flesh of the fish registers an internal temperature of 135-140 degrees F. Remove fish from the grill and let stand 10 minutes.
4. Using a wooden spoon, strike the crust to crack it open and brush remaining salt from the surface of the fish.
5. Remove the skin and drizzle fish with good olive oil and a squeeze of lemon. Enjoy!

Oysters In The Shell

Servings: 4
Cooking Time: 20 Minutes

Ingredients:
- 8 medium oysters, unopened, in the shell, rinsed and scrubbed
- 1 batch Lemon Butter Mop for Seafood

Directions:
1. Supply your smoker with wood pellets and follow the start-up procedure. Preheat the grill, with the lid closed, to 375°F.

2. Place the unopened oysters directly on the grill grate and grill for about 20 minutes, or until the oysters are done and their shells open.
3. Discard any oysters that do not open. Shuck the remaining oysters, transfer them to a bowl, and add the mop. Serve immediately.

Lobster Tail

Servings: 2
Cooking Time: 25 Minutes

Ingredients:
- 2 lobster tails
- Salt
- Freshly ground black pepper
- 1 batch Lemon Butter Mop for Seafood

Directions:
1. Supply your smoker with wood pellets and follow the start-up procedure. Preheat the grill, with the lid closed, to 375°F.
2. Using kitchen shears, slit the top of the lobster shells, through the center, nearly to the tail. Once cut, expose as much meat as you can through the cut shell.
3. Season the lobster tails all over with salt and pepper.
4. Place the tails directly on the grill grate and grill until their internal temperature reaches 145°F. Remove the lobster from the grill and serve with the mop on the side for dipping.

Grilled Blackened Saskatchewan Salmon

Servings: 4
Cooking Time: 30 Minutes

Ingredients:
- 1 salmon fillets
- zesty Italian dressing
- Blackened Saskatchewan Rub
- lemon wedges

Directions:
1. Brush salmon with Italian dressing and season with Traeger Blackened Saskatchewan Rub.
2. Supply your smoker with wood pellets and follow the start-up procedure. Preheat the grill, with the lid closed, to 325° F.
3. Place salmon on the grill and cook for 20 to 30 minutes, until it reaches an internal temperature of 145°F and flakes easily. Remove salmon from grill. Serve with lemon wedges. Enjoy! Grill: 325 °F Probe: 145 °F

Sweet Smoked Salmon Jerky

Servings: 6
Cooking Time: 300 Minutes

Ingredients:
- 2 Quart water
- 3/4 Cup kosher salt
- 1 Cup Morton Tender Quick Home Meat Cure, optional
- 4 Cup dark brown sugar
- 2 Cup maple syrup, divided
- 1 (2-3 lb) wild caught salmon fillet, skinned and pin bones removed

Directions:
1. In a large nonreactive bowl, combine 2 quarts water, salt, curing salt (if using), brown sugar and 1 cup of the maple syrup. Stir with a long-handled spoon to dissolve the salts and sugar.
2. With a sharp, serrated knife, slice the salmon into 1/2 inch thick slices with the short side parallel to you on the cutting board. In other words, make your cuts from the head end to the tail end. (This is considerably easier if the fish is frozen.) Cut each strip crosswise into 4 or 5 inch lengths.
3. Immerse the strips in the brine, weighing down with a plate or a bag of ice. Cover with plastic wrap and refrigerate for 12 hours.

4. Supply your smoker with wood pellets and follow the start-up procedure. Preheat the grill, with the lid closed, to 180° F.

5. Drain the salmon strips and discard the brine. Arrange the salmon strips in a single layer directly on the grill grate. Smoke for several hours (5 to 6), or until the jerky is dry but not rock-hard. You want it to yield when you bite into it. Halfway through the smoking time, mix the remaining cup of maple syrup with 1/4 cup of warm water and brush the salmon strips on all sides with the mixture. Grill: 180 °F

6. Transfer to a resealable bag while the jerky is still warm. Let the jerky rest for an hour at room temperature. Squeeze any air from the bag, and refrigerate the jerky. Enjoy!

Honey Balsamic Salmon

Servings: 2
Cooking Time: 25 Minutes

Ingredients:
- 1 Medium salmon fillet
- Fin & Feather Rub
- 1/2 Cup balsamic vinegar
- 1 Tablespoon minced garlic
- 2 Tablespoon honey

Directions:
1. Season the fillet with the Traeger Fin & Feather Rub.
2. Make the glaze: Combine the vinegar, garlic and honey in a small saucepan. Simmer over medium heat until reduced by half. Usually 10 to 15 minutes. The glaze will be properly reduced when it coats the back of a spoon. Using a basting brush, coat the fillet with the glaze.
3. Supply your smoker with wood pellets and follow the start-up procedure. Preheat the grill, with the lid closed, to 350° F.
4. Arrange the salmon fillet on the grill grate. Grill for 25 to 30 minutes, or until the salmon is opaque and flakes easily with a fork. Grill: 350 °F
5. Transfer to a platter or plates and serve immediately. If desired, heat any remaining glaze to a boil and drizzle over top of the salmon. Enjoy!

Spicy Crab Poppers

Servings: 8
Cooking Time: 30 Minutes

Ingredients:
- 18 Whole jalapeño
- 8 Ounce cream cheese, softened
- 1 Cup Canned Corn, drained
- 1/2 Cup Crab meat, lump
- 1 1/4 Teaspoon Old Bay Seasoning
- 2 Scallions, minced

Directions:
1. Cut each jalapeño in half lengthwise through the stem and remove the ribs and seeds.
2. Filling: In a mixing bowl, combine the cream cheese, corn, crab meat, scallions, and Old Bay Seasoning and stir until blended. Stir in the scallions. Spoon the filling into the jalapeño halves, mounding it slightly.
3. Arrange the poppers on a baking sheet covered with foil or parchment paper.
4. Supply your smoker with wood pellets and follow the start-up procedure. Preheat the grill, with the lid closed, to 350° F.
5. Roast the jalapeños for 25 to 30 minutes, or until the peppers have softened and the filling is hot and bubbling.
6. Let cool slightly before serving. Enjoy!

PORK RECIPES

Whiskey- & Cider-brined Pork Shoulder

Servings: 8
Cooking Time: 540 Minutes

Ingredients:
- 1 bone-in pork shoulder, about 5 to 7lb (2.3 to 3.2kg)
- fresh coarsely ground black pepper
- granulated garlic
- 1 cup apple juice or apple cider
- low-carb barbecue sauce, warmed
- hamburger buns (optional)
- for the brine
- 1 gallon (3.8 liters) cold distilled water
- 1 cup coarse salt
- 1¼ cup whiskey, divided
- ½ cup light brown sugar or low-carb substitute

Directions:
1. In a large saucepot on the stovetop over medium-high heat, make the brine by bringing the water, salt, 1 cup of whiskey, and brown sugar to a boil. Stir with a long-handled wooden spoon until the salt and sugar dissolve. Let the brine cool to room temperature. Cover and cool completely in the refrigerator.
2. Submerge the pork in the brine. If it floats, place a resealable bag of ice on top. Refrigerate for 24 hours.
3. Supply your smoker with wood pellets and follow the start-up procedure. Preheat the grill, with the lid closed, to 250° F.
4. Remove the pork shoulder from the brine and pat dry with paper towels. (Discard the brine.) Season the pork with pepper and granulated garlic. Place the pork on the grate and smoke until the internal temperature reaches 165°F (74°C), about 5 hours.
5. Transfer the pork to an aluminum foil roasting pan and add the apple juice and the remaining ¼ cup of whiskey. Cover tightly with aluminum foil. Place the pan on the grate and cook the pork until the bone releases easily from the meat and the internal temperature reaches 200°F (93°C), about 3 hours more. (Be careful when lifting a corner of the foil to check on the roast because steam will escape.)
6. Remove the pan from the grill and let the pork rest for 20 minutes. Reserve the juices.
7. Wearing heatproof gloves, pull the pork into chunks. Discard the bone or any large lumps of fat. Pull the meat into shreds and transfer to a clean aluminum foil roasting pan. Moisten with the barbecue sauce or serve the sauce on the side. Stir in some of the drippings—not too much because you don't want the pork to be swimming in its juices. Serve on buns (if using).

Pork Tenderloin

Servings: 2
Cooking Time: 15 Minutes

Ingredients:
- 1 Pound pork tenderloin
- 1/3 Cup Kentucky bourbon or apple juice
- 1/4 Cup low sodium soy sauce
- 1/4 Cup brown sugar, packed
- 2 Tablespoon Dijon mustard

- 2 Teaspoon Worcestershire sauce
- 1 Teaspoon ground black pepper
- 1 Medium onion, chopped
- 2 Clove garlic, minced

Directions:
1. Trim any silverskin from the tenderloins with a sharp knife. Place meat in a large resealable plastic bag.
2. For the marinade: In a small mixing bowl or resealable bag, combine the bourbon, soy sauce, brown sugar, mustard, Worcestershire sauce and pepper, whisk to mix. Stir in the onion and garlic. Pour over the tenderloins and refrigerate for 8 hours or overnight.
3. Supply your smoker with wood pellets and follow the start-up procedure. Preheat the grill, with the lid closed, to 400° F.
4. Remove the pork from the marinade and scrape off any solid ingredients (onion or bits of garlic). Discard the marinade.
5. Arrange the tenderloins on the grill grate and grill for 6 to 8 minutes per side or until the internal temperature is 145°F. The pork will still be slightly pink in the center. If you prefer your pork well-done, cook it to 160°F. Grill: 400 °F Probe: 145 °F
6. Transfer the tenderloins to a cutting board. Let rest for several minutes before carving on a diagonal into 1/2 inch slices. Enjoy!

Bbq Sweet & Smoky Ribs

Servings: 6
Cooking Time: 300 Minutes

Ingredients:
- 2 Rack Pork, Spare Ribs Trimmed
- 6 Cup apple juice
- 2 Tablespoon Big Game Rub
- 2 Cup 'Que BBQ Sauce
- 1/4 Cup brown sugar

Directions:
1. If your butcher has not already done so, remove the thin papery membrane from the bone-side of the ribs by working the tip of a butter knife underneath the membrane over a middle bone. Use paper towels to get a firm grip, then tear the membrane off.
2. Lay the ribs in a baking dish. Pour the apple juice over ribs, using as much apple juice as needed to submerge the meaty side of the ribs. Turn to coat.
3. Cover and refrigerate ribs for 4 to 6 hours or overnight. Remove the ribs from the apple juice; reserve juice.
4. Sprinkle ribs on all sides with Traeger Big Game Rub.
5. Supply your smoker with wood pellets and follow the start-up procedure. Preheat the grill, with the lid closed, to 225° F.
6. Transfer the apple juice to a saucepan and place in a corner of the grill, the juice will keep the cooking environment moist.
7. Arrange the ribs bone side down, directly on the grill grate. Cook for 4 to 5 hours, or until a skewer or paring knife inserted between the bones goes in easily.
8. Check the internal temperature of the ribs, the desired temperature is 202°F. If not at temperature, cook for an additional 30 minutes or until temperature is reached.
9. Meanwhile, combine the BBQ sauce and brown sugar in a small saucepan. Generously brush the ribs on all sides with the BBQ sauce the last hour of cooking
10. Using a sharp knife, cut the slabs into individual ribs. Serve. Enjoy!

Spiced Pulled Pork Shoulder

Servings: 16
Cooking Time: 600 Minutes

Ingredients:
- 5-8 lb Bone-in Pork Shoulder
- Maple Chili Rub
- Maple Sugar
- Kosher Salt
- Fresh Ground Black Pepper
- Roasted Garlic Powder
- Onion Powder
- Cumin
- Chipotle Powder
- Chili Powder
- Cinnamon Powder

Directions:
1. Supply your smoker with wood pellets and follow the start-up procedure. Preheat the grill, with the lid closed, to 225° F. Using apple pellets for this dish will impart a slightly sweeter smoke that goes great with the rub.
2. In a bowl combine rub ingredients.
3. Trim excess fat from pork shoulder, score fat with a sharp knife (only slice about 1/8" into pork), then cover with rub. Reserve some rub to be sprinkled on the meat after it has been shredded.
4. Place the pork onto the smoker.
5. Continue to smoke pork until internal temperature reaches 203 °F, about 10 hours. You can wrap pork in butcher paper once it reaches 160 °F if you want to speed up cooking time (your final bark won't be as good though).
6. Once Pork reaches 203 °F, remove from smoker then wrap tightly in aluminum foil. Place wrapped Pork into a cooler for 1 hour.
7. After 1 hour remove pork from the foil, pull out the bones, using 2 forks shred the pork to your desired consistency.
8. Sprinkle left over rub onto the pork and toss to coat.
9. Enjoy!

Smoked Bacon Roses

Servings: 2
Cooking Time: 60 Minutes

Ingredients:
- 1 Pack Bacon, Thick Cut
- 1 Dozen Roses, Fake

Directions:
1. Supply your smoker with wood pellets and follow the start-up procedure. Preheat the grill, with the lid open, to 225° F.
2. Roll each piece of bacon tightly, starting on the thicker side of the strip. Take a toothpick and skewer the middle of the bottom of the bacon roll to keep the bacon from unraveling. With a second toothpick, skewer the bacon roll so that the two toothpicks form an "X" at the bottom of the roll of bacon. Do this to every piece of bacon.
3. Place the bacon rolls directly on the grates of your preheated Grill and smoke for an hour, checking on them every 20 minutes.
4. While the bacon is smoking, rip the petals of the fake roses off of the steams.
5. Once the bacon is fully cooked, remove the toothpicks and pierce the bacon in the head of the steam (where the fake flowers once were). If the bacon isn't staying, you can break a toothpick in half and stick it in the tip of the steam, press firmly and try piercing the bacon again.
6. Place in a nice vase with some babies breath and gift to your Valentine.

Grilled Sweet Pork Tenderloin

Servings: 4
Cooking Time: 20 Minutes

Ingredients:
- 2 Tablespoons Brown Sugar
- 2 Tablespoons Olive Oil
- 2 Tablespoons Tennessee Apple Butter Seasoning
- 1 Pork Tenderloin, Trimmed With Silver Skins Removed

Directions:
1. In a small bowl, combine the olive oil, brown sugar, and Tennessee Apple Butter seasoning until well combined. Generously rub the pork tenderloin with the mixture. Allow the pork tenderloin to marinade for 1 hour.
2. Supply your smoker with wood pellets and follow the start-up procedure. Preheat the grill, with the lid open, to 350° F.
3. Grill the tenderloin for 5-7 minutes on each side, flipping the tenderloin only once and cooking until the internal temperature reaches 140-145°F.
4. Remove the tenderloin from the grill and allow to rest 10 minutes before slicing and serving.

Pickle Brined Grilled Pork Chops

Servings: 4
Cooking Time: 60 Minutes

Ingredients:
- 4 pork chops
- 3 Cup Dill Pickle Brine, jar
- coarse ground black pepper, divided

Directions:
1. Put the pork chops and pickle brine in a resealable plastic bag. Refrigerate for at least 4 hours. Drain well and pat dry with paper towels.
2. Season generously with black pepper.
3. Supply your smoker with wood pellets and follow the start-up procedure. Preheat the grill, with the lid closed, to 300° F.
4. Put the chops directly on the grill grate and grill, turning once, for about 1 hour, or until the internal temperature of the chop is at least 145°F. Grill: 300 °F Probe: 145 °F
5. Let rest for 5 minutes before serving. Enjoy!

Sweet And Spicy Pork Roast

Servings: 2
Cooking Time: 60 Minutes

Ingredients:
- 2 Pound Pork, Loins
- 2/3 habanero peppers, seeded
- 2/3 Can coconut milk
- 1/3 Teaspoon Chinese five-spice powder
- 2/3 Tablespoon paprika
- 2/3 Teaspoon curry powder
- 2/3 Tablespoon lime juice
- 2/3 Tablespoon garlic, minced
- 2/3 Teaspoon freshly grated ginger

Directions:
1. Mix all ingredients, except pork, in a bowl. Rub the mixture onto your pork and let it sit overnight.
2. Supply your smoker with wood pellets and follow the start-up procedure. Preheat the grill, with the lid closed, to 300° F.
3. Place pork on hot grill. Cook for 1 to 1-1/2 hours, or until it reaches an internal temperature of 145-150°F for medium-rare to medium. Enjoy! Grill: 300 °F Probe: 150 °F

Apple-smoked Pork Tenderloin

Servings: 4-6
Cooking Time: 300 Minutes

Ingredients:
- 2 (1-pound) pork tenderloins
- 1 batch Pork Rub

Directions:
1. Supply your smoker with wood pellets and follow the start-up procedure. Preheat the grill, with the lid closed, to 180°F.
2. Generously season the tenderloins with the rub. Using your hands, work the rub into the meat.
3. Place the tenderloins directly on the grill grate and smoke for 4 or 5 hours, until their internal temperature reaches 145°F.
4. Remove the tenderloins from the grill and let them rest for 5 to 10 minutes before thinly slicing and serving.

Bbq Breakfast Grits

Servings: 12-15
Cooking Time: 40 Minutes

Ingredients:
- 2 cups chicken stock
- 1 cup water
- 1 cup quick-cooking grits
- 3 tablespoons unsalted butter
- 2 tablespoons minced garlic
- 1 medium onion, chopped
- 1 jalapeño pepper, stemmed, seeded, and chopped
- 1 teaspoon cayenne pepper
- 2 teaspoons red pepper flakes
- 1 tablespoon hot sauce
- 1 cup shredded Monterey Jack cheese
- 1 cup sour cream
- Salt
- Freshly ground black pepper
- 2 eggs, beaten
- ⅓ cup half-and-half
- 3 cups leftover pulled pork (preferably smoked

Directions:
1. Supply your smoker with wood pellets and follow the start-up procedure. Preheat, with the lid closed, to 350°F.
2. On your kitchen stove top, in a large saucepan over high heat, bring the chicken stock and water to a boil.
3. Add the grits and reduce the heat to low, then stir in the butter, garlic, onion, jalapeño, cayenne, red pepper flakes, hot sauce, cheese, and sour cream. Season with salt and pepper, then cook for about 5 minutes.
4. Temper the beaten eggs (see Tip below) and incorporate into the grits. Remove the saucepan from the heat and stir in the half-and-half and pulled pork.
5. Pour the grits into a greased grill-safe 9-by-13-inch casserole dish or aluminum pan.
6. Transfer to the grill, close the lid, and bake for 30 to 40 minutes, covering with aluminum foil toward the end of cooking if the grits start to get too brown on top.

Smoked Rendezvous Ribs

Servings: 4
Cooking Time: 120 Minutes

Ingredients:
- 1/2 Cup apple cider vinegar
- 1/2 Cup water
- 1/2 Cup BBQ Sauce
- 2 Tablespoon Pork & Poultry Rub

- 3 Rack baby back pork ribs, membrane removed
- 1 As Needed Pork & Poultry Rub

Directions:

1. In a mixing bowl, combine vinegar, water, barbecue sauce, and Traeger Pork and Poultry rub. Set the sauce and a barbecue mop or basting brush grill-side.
2. Supply your smoker with wood pellets and follow the start-up procedure. Preheat the grill, with the lid closed, to 325° F.
3. Arrange the ribs on the grill grate, meat-side up.
4. Grill for 30 minutes, then start mopping. Mop every 15 minutes. After 2 hours, check the ribs for doneness. Grill: 325 °F
5. Insert a toothpick between the bones in the center of a rack. If there is little or no resistance, the ribs are done (or close to it). If the ribs are not to your liking, continue to grill them in 30-minute increments, mopping every 15 minutes. Grill: 325 °F
6. When the ribs are done, transfer them to a cutting board and give them a final dose of the mop sauce. Sprinkle lightly with Traeger Pork and Poultry Rub.
7. Let the ribs rest for a few minutes before cutting into half slabs or individual ribs. Enjoy!

Grilled Raspberry Chipotle Pork Ribs

Servings: 4
Cooking Time: 180 Minutes

Ingredients:

- Baby Back Rib
- Original Bbq Sauce
- Raspberry Chipotle Spice Rub

Directions:

1. Begin by gently rinsing off your ribs in cool water. Pat dry and remove the flavor blocker (thin membrane on the underside of the ribs) to allow the seasoning to permeate right into the meat.
2. Generously season your ribs with Raspberry Chipotle seasoning and place in the refrigerator for an hour for flavor to set in.
3. Supply your smoker with wood pellets and follow the start-up procedure. Preheat the grill, with the lid open, to 250° F. Place your seasoned rack of ribs on the grill and let cook for 2 hours. Next, lather on a thick coating of Original BBQ Sauce, turn up the grill to 300°F and let your ribs roast for another hour. Remove, cut and serve for a meal that will surely make its way into the weekly rotation.

Onion Pork Shoulder

Servings: 8 - 10
Cooking Time: 240 Minutes

Ingredients:

- Aluminum Foil
- 1 Diced Apple
- 1 Cup Broth, Chicken
- 2 Tbsp Butter, Salted
- 1 Diced Onion
- 1 Pork Shoulder Or Pork Butt Roast
- 1 Box Or Bag Of Stovetop Stuffing Mix
- Champion Chicken Seasoning

Directions:

1. Prepare the pork shoulder. Place the pork shoulder on the cutting board, and with a sharp knife, trim any very fatty sections of the pork shoulder and remove. Then, butterfly the shoulder. Beginning on one side, carefully cut a slit horizontally into one side of the pork shoulder

and carefully continue to slice almost all the way to the right side, rolling the shoulder as you cut, unfolding the meat like a book, until the pork shoulder is one long strip.

2. Began to make the stuffing by using a medium sized pan and adding 2 tbsp of salted butter to the pan. Add in the onion and apple and let cook for about 5 minutes making sure to stir in between. Add 2 tbsp of Champion Chicken Seasoning. Add the 1 cup of chicken broth followed by a bag of stuffing mix. Let reduce and mix together very well and remove from heat. Transfer to a bowl and set aside.

3. Once the pork shoulder is butterflied, place some stuff on the roast making sure to leave enough space to roll and tie the roast as well.

4. Starting on one end of the pork shoulder, roll the pork shoulder up into a tight spiral, and set onto the cutting board, seam side down. Cut four even lengths of butcher's twine, and wiggle under the pork shoulder, two inches apart from each other. Tie tightly to hold the roast together and place on a sheet pan.

5. Supply your smoker with wood pellets and follow the start-up procedure. Preheat the grill, with the lid open, to 250° F. If you're using a gas or charcoal grill, set it up for medium low heat. Place the aluminum pan in the center of the grill and cook for 3-4 hours, or until the temperature of the pork shoulder reaches an internal temperature of 180°F and is very tender.

6. Remove the pork shoulder from the grill and allow to rest for 15 minutes, then slice and serve.

Smoked Chili Con Queso By Doug Scheiding

Servings: 8

Cooking Time: 45 Minutes

Ingredients:
- 1 Pound hot pork sausage
- 1 (2 lb) block Velveeta cheese
- 1 Pound smoked Gouda cheese
- 1 (10 oz) can RO*TEL Original Diced Tomatoes and Green Chilies
- 1 (10 oz) can RO*TEL Fire Roasted Diced Tomatoes and Green Chilies
- 1 (10 oz) can cream of mushroom soup
- 4 Tablespoon Coffee Rub
- 1/2 Cup chopped cilantro

Directions:
1. Heat a medium cast iron skillet over medium heat and fully cook pork sausage, breaking into small chunks as you go. Remove the sausage and drain and discard the fat.

2. Supply your smoker with wood pellets and follow the start-up procedure. Preheat the grill, with the lid closed, to 350° F.

3. Use a 4 to 5 quart cast iron Dutch oven or other oven safe dish. Divide the block of Velveeta into 5 to 6 large pieces and cut the smoked Gouda into small 1 inch cubes. Add the canned ingredients including the liquid. Add the sausage and Traeger Coffee Rub last. Grill: 350 °F

4. Smoke the queso for 45 minutes on the Traeger, stirring 3 to 4 times. Grill: 350 °F

5. Add most of the cilantro the last 5 minutes of smoking. Sprinkle remaining cilantro on the top before serving. Enjoy!

Pork Belly Burnt Ends

Servings: 8-10
Cooking Time: 360 Minutes

Ingredients:

- 1 (3-pound) skinless pork belly (if not already skinned, use a sharp boning knife to remove the skin from the belly), cut into 1½- to 2-inch cubes
- 1 batch Sweet Brown Sugar Rub
- ½ cup honey
- 1 cup The Ultimate BBQ Sauce
- 2 tablespoons light brown sugar

Directions:

1. Supply your smoker with wood pellets and follow the start-up procedure. Preheat the grill, with the lid closed, to 250°F.
2. Generously season the pork belly cubes with the rub. Using your hands, work the rub into the meat.
3. Place the pork cubes directly on the grill grate and smoke until their internal temperature reaches 195°F.
4. Transfer the cubes from the grill to an aluminum pan. Add the honey, barbecue sauce, and brown sugar. Stir to combine and coat the pork.
5. Place the pan in the grill and smoke the pork for 1 hour, uncovered. Remove the pork from the grill and serve immediately.

St. Louis Bbq Ribs

Servings: 4
Cooking Time: 240 Minutes

Ingredients:

- 2 Rack St. Louis-style ribs
- 1/4 Cup Pork & Poultry Rub
- 1 Cup apple juice
- 1 Bottle Sweet & Heat BBQ Sauce

Directions:

1. Trim ribs and peel off membrane from the back of ribs. Apply an even coat of rub to the front and back of ribs. Let sit for 20 minutes and up to 4 hours if refrigerated.
2. Supply your smoker with wood pellets and follow the start-up procedure. Preheat the grill, with the lid closed, to 225° F.
3. Place ribs bone side down on grill grate. Put apple juice in a spray bottle and evenly spray ribs. Grill: 225 °F
4. After 3 hours, remove ribs from grill and wrap them in aluminum foil. Leave an opening at one end, pour in remainder of apple juice (about 6 oz) into the foil and wrap tightly.
5. Place ribs back on grill, meat side down and smoke for an additional 3 hours. Grill: 225 °F Probe: 203 °F
6. After 1 hour, start checking the internal temperature of ribs. Ribs are done when the internal temperature reaches 203°F. Grill: 225 °F
7. When ribs are done, remove from the foil and brush a light layer of sauce on the front and back on the ribs.
8. Return to the grill and cook an additional 10 minutes to set the sauce. Grill: 225 °F
9. After sauce has set, take ribs off the grill and let rest for 10 minutes. To serve, slice ribs in between the bones. Enjoy!

Anytime Pork Roast

Servings: 6
Cooking Time: 360 Minutes

Ingredients:

- 6 (4-6 lb) pork roast
- Pork & Poultry Rub

- 1/4 Cup apple juice

Directions:
1. Supply your smoker with wood pellets and follow the start-up procedure. Preheat the grill, with the lid closed, to 180° F.
2. Sprinkle pork roast with Traeger Pork & Poultry Rub on all sides. Place roast in an aluminum foil pan and pour apple juice on top. Place roast in the grill and smoke the for 1 hour. Grill: 180 °F
3. Remove roast from grill and increase Traeger temperature to 275°F and preheat, lid closed 15 minutes. Grill: 275 °F
4. Cook roast for an additional 2 hours, uncovered. After two hours, wrap pan with aluminum foil and return to grill to cook for an additional 3 hours or until the internal temperature reaches 205°F. Grill: 275 °F Probe: 205 °F
5. Allow to rest for 10 minutes before serving. Serve with roasted onions, potatoes, carrots and apples. Enjoy!

Apple Bacon Smoked Ham

Servings: 8-12
Cooking Time: 120 Minutes

Ingredients:
- 1 1/2 Cup Apple Cider
- 3 Tablespoon Apple Cider Vinegar
- 2 Apples
- 1 Lb. Bacon
- 2 Tablespoon Butter, Unsalted
- 2 Tablespoon Cornstarch
- 3 Tablespoon Dijon Mustard
- Smoke Infused Applewood Bacon Rub
- 1/2 Cup Pure Maple Syrup
- 1 Large Bone In Spiral Cut Smoked Ham
- 2 Tablespoon Yellow Mustard

Directions:
1. Supply your smoker with wood pellets and follow the start-up procedure. Preheat the grill, with the lid open, to 250° F.
2. Smoke the bacon directly on the grates for 25 minutes, flipping at the 15-minute mark. Thinly slice the apples while the bacon cooks. Once the bacon is done, set your temperature down to 225 degrees F.
3. Put the spiral-sliced ham into an aluminum foil roasting pan. Start by adding apple into the first slice and every other slice after that. Fill in all other slices with the bacon strips. Season with Smoke Infused Applewood Bacon Rub. Add any extra apple cider to the bottom of the pan for added flavor.
4. Place ham in the grill for 60 minutes.
5. Meanwhile, in a saucepan, whisk together apple cider, maple syrup, apple cider vinegar, Dijon mustard, yellow mustard, cornstarch and Smoke Infused Applewood Bacon Rub. Bring to a boil. Reduce to a simmer, stirring often, until the sauce has thickened and reduced (approximately 15-20 minutes). Stir in the butter until it has completely melted. Glaze should thicken more as it stands.
6. After 60 minutes, add carrots into the roasting pan and glaze the entire ham. Glaze again every 30 minutes until done.
7. Remove ham from grill and allow to rest covered with foil for 20 minutes before serving.
8. Serve with remaining warmed up sauce if desired.

Smoked Pig Shots

Servings: 8
Cooking Time: 45 Minutes

Ingredients:
- 1 (8 oz) block cream cheese, softened
- 2 Large green chile peppers, diced
- 1 Cup shredded cheese
- 1 Tablespoon chile powder
- 2 Tablespoon Meat Church Honey Hog BBQ Rub
- 1 Pound Sausage, Smoked
- 1 Pound thick-cut bacon

Directions:
1. Supply your smoker with wood pellets and follow the start-up procedure. Preheat the grill, with the lid closed, to 350° F.
2. Mix cream cheese, chiles, shredded cheese, chili powder and Honey Hog BBQ Rub thoroughly in a mixing bowl. Set aside.
3. Slice sausage into 1/2 inch slices. Cut bacon strips in half. Wrap bacon around the sausage, creating a bowl and secure with a toothpick.
4. Fill the bowl with the cream cheese mixture. Top with more Honey Hog BBQ Rub.
5. Place the pig shots on the Traeger until the bacon is crispy and golden brown, about 45 to 60 minutes. Grill: 350 °F
6. Remove the pig shots from the grill and cool for 10 minutes, the cream cheese may still be hot. Enjoy!

Grilled Pork Belly

Servings: 15
Cooking Time: 370 Minutes

Ingredients:
- Peanut Oil
- Mandarin Habanero Spice
- 13 Lbs Pork, Belly (Skin And Fat)
- Salt
- Sweet Barbecue Sauce

Directions:
1. Supply your smoker with wood pellets and follow the start-up procedure. Preheat the grill, with the lid open, to 250° F.
2. Place the pork belly on the grates of your preheated , meat side down. Smoke until the internal temperature reaches 195°F (this normally takes about 6 hours).
3. Open the flame broiler and flip the pork belly so that the meat side is up. Brush on the BBQ Sauce (on meat side). Sear the fat side for about 5 minutes, or until crispy.
4. Using your grill gloves, remove the pork belly from the grill and wrap in aluminum foil for 15 minutes or until it's cool enough to pull apart with your Meat Claws. Or dice into cubes with a knife. Serve hot.

3-2-1 Spare Ribs

Servings: 4
Cooking Time: 180 Minutes

Ingredients:
- 2 racks of St. Louis–cut pork spare ribs, each about 3lb (1.4kg)
- all-purpose barbecue rub
- 3 tbsp unsalted butter, cut into cubes
- 1 cup apple juice or apple cider
- low-carb barbecue sauce

Directions:
1. Supply your smoker with wood pellets and follow the start-up procedure. Preheat the grill, with the lid closed, to 225° F.

2. Place the ribs on a rimmed sheet pan and dust with the rub. Place the ribs bone side down on the grate and smoke for 3 hours.
3. Tear off 2 large sheets of heavy-duty aluminum foil. Place one rack of ribs bone side down on the foil and top with half the butter cubes. Place the second rack of ribs bone side down on the butter cubes and top with the remaining butter cubes.
4. Bring up all 4 sides of the foil and pour in the apple juice. Crimp the edges of the foil so the ribs are tightly enclosed. Place the foil package on the grate and smoke for 2 hours more.
5. Transfer the ribs to a workspace and carefully open the foil package. (Be careful of escaping steam.) Discard the foil and any accumulated juices. Brush the ribs on both sides with barbecue sauce. Place the ribs on the grate and smoke for 1 hour more to set the sauce and firm up the bark.
6. Transfer the ribs to a cutting board. Use a sharp knife to cut the slabs in half or into individual ribs. Serve immediately.

Baked Candied Bacon Cinnamon Rolls

Servings: 6
Cooking Time: 35 Minutes

Ingredients:
- 12 Slices Bacon, sliced
- 1/3 Cup brown sugar
- pre-made cinnamon rolls
- 2 Ounce cream cheese

Directions:
1. Supply your smoker with wood pellets and follow the start-up procedure. Preheat the grill, with the lid closed, to 350° F.
2. Dredge 8 of the slices of bacon in brown sugar, making sure to cover both sides of the bacon.
3. Place the brown sugared bacon slices along with the other slices of bacon on a cooling rack placed on top of a large baking sheet.
4. Cook the bacon on the Traeger for 15-20 minutes or until the fat renders but bacon is still pliable. Turn the Traeger down to 325°F.
5. Open and unroll the cinnamon rolls. While bacon is still warm, place 1 slice of the brown sugared bacon on top of 1 of the unrolled rolls and roll back up. Repeat for all the rolls.
6. Place cinnamon rolls in an 8" x 8" baking dish or cake pan that has been sprayed with nonstick cooking spray. Cook the cinnamon rolls at 325°F for 10 to 15 minutes or until golden. Rotate the pan a half turn halfway through cooking time. Grill: 325 °F
7. Meanwhile, take the provided cream cheese frosting and mix in the softened cream cheese. Crumble the cooked bacon and add into the cream cheese frosting.
8. Spread frosting over warm cinnamon rolls. Serve warm, enjoy!

Balsamic Brussels Sprouts With Bacon

Servings: 8
Cooking Time: 25 Minutes

Ingredients:
- 6 Strips thick-cut bacon
- 2 Pound Brussels sprouts, trimmed and halved
- 1 Small onion, diced
- 2 Tablespoon olive oil or vegetable oil
- freshly ground black pepper

- salt
- 1/2 Cup chicken stock
- 1 Tablespoon balsamic vinegar

Directions:

1. Supply your smoker with wood pellets and follow the start-up procedure. Preheat the grill, with the lid closed, to 450° F.
2. Place the bacon strips directly on the grill grate and cook for 20 minutes. Grill: 450 °F
3. Line a large baking sheet with foil for easy cleanup. Place the onion and sprouts cut-side down on the baking sheet, drizzle with oil and season with salt and pepper.
4. Place the baking sheet directly on the grill grate next to the bacon and roast until they turn a light golden brown, about 8 to 10 minutes. Grill: 450 °F
5. Add the cooked bacon, pour chicken stock and balsamic vinegar over the sprouts, mix and continue to cook until the liquid has thickened. Remove from heat. Enjoy!

Southern Sugar-glazed Ham

Servings: 12-15
Cooking Time: 300 Minutes

Ingredients:

- 1 (12- to 15-pound) whole bone-in ham, fully cooked
- ¼ cup yellow mustard
- 1 cup pineapple juice
- ½ cup packed light brown sugar
- 1 teaspoon ground cinnamon
- ½ teaspoon ground cloves

Directions:

1. Supply your smoker with wood pellets and follow the start-up procedure. Preheat, with the lid closed, to 275°F.
2. Trim off the excess fat and skin from the ham, leaving a ¼-inch layer of fat. Put the ham in an aluminum foil–lined roasting pan.
3. On your kitchen stove top, in a medium saucepan over low heat, combine the mustard, pineapple juice, brown sugar, cinnamon, and cloves and simmer for 15 minutes, or until thick and reduced by about half.
4. Baste the ham with half of the pineapple–brown sugar syrup, reserving the rest for basting later in the cook.
5. Place the roasting pan on the grill, close the lid, and smoke for 4 hours.
6. Baste the ham with the remaining pineapple–brown sugar syrup and continue smoking with the lid closed for another hour, or until a meat thermometer inserted in the thickest part of the ham reads 140°F.
7. Remove the ham from the grill, tent with foil, and let rest for 20 minutes before carving.

Smoked Pork Loin With Sauerkraut And Apples

Servings: 4
Cooking Time: 120 Minutes

Ingredients:

- 1 (2 to 2-1/2 lb) pork loin roast
- Pork & Poultry Rub
- 1 Pound sauerkraut
- 2 Large cooking apples, peeled, cored and sliced
- 1 Large sweet onion, thinly sliced
- 1/3 Cup brown sugar
- 1 Cup dark beer
- 2 Tablespoon butter
- 2 Whole bay leaves

Directions:

1. Supply your smoker with wood pellets and follow the start-up procedure. Preheat the grill, with the lid closed, to 180° F.
2. Season the pork loin on all sides with Traeger Pork & Poultry Rub or salt and pepper. Place the roast directly on the grill grate, close the lid, and smoke for 1 hour. Grill: 180 °F
3. In a large Dutch oven or glass baking dish, layer the sauerkraut, apples, onions, brown sugar, beer, butter and bay leaves. Lay the smoked pork loin directly on top of the sauerkraut mixture. Top the pan with a lid or a layer of foil.
4. Increase Traeger temperature to 350°F, and return the pan to the grill. Close the lid and roast the pork for an additional hour, or until the internal temperature on an instant-read meat thermometer reads 160°F. Grill: 350 °F Probe: 160 °F
5. Transfer the roast to a cutting board and let it rest. Meanwhile, gently stir the sauerkraut mixture and arrange on a serving platter. Slice the pork roast and layer on the sauerkraut and apples. Enjoy!

Smoked Ham

Servings: 12-15
Cooking Time: 300 Minutes

Ingredients:
- 1 (10-pound) fresh ham, skin removed
- 2 tablespoons olive oil
- 1 batch Rosemary-Garlic Lamb Seasoning

Directions:
1. Supply your smoker with wood pellets and follow the start-up procedure. Preheat the grill, with the lid closed, to 180°F.
2. Rub the ham all over with olive oil and sprinkle it with the seasoning.
3. Place the ham directly on the grill grate and smoke for 3 hours.
4. Increase the grill's temperature to 375°F and continue to smoke the ham until its internal temperature reaches 170°F.
5. Remove the ham from the grill and let it rest for 10 minutes, before carving and serving.

VEGETABLES RECIPES

Smoked Jalapeño Poppers

Servings: 4
Cooking Time: 60 Minutes

Ingredients:

- 12 Medium jalapeño
- 6 Slices bacon, cut in half
- 8 Ounce cream cheese
- 2 Tablespoon Pork & Poultry Rub
- 1 Cup grated cheese

Directions:

1. Supply your smoker with wood pellets and follow the start-up procedure. Preheat the grill, with the lid closed, to 180° F. For optimal flavor, use Super Smoke if available.
2. Slice the jalapeños in half lengthwise. Scrape out any seeds and ribs with a small spoon or paring knife. Mix softened cream cheese with Traeger Pork & Poultry rub and grated cheese. Spoon mixture onto each jalapeño half. Wrap with bacon and secure with a toothpick.
3. Place the jalapeños on a rimmed baking sheet. Place on grill and smoke for 30 minutes. Grill: 180 °F
4. Increase the grill temperature to 375°F and cook an additional 30 minutes or until bacon is cooked to desired doneness. Serve warm, enjoy! Grill: 375 °F

Roasted Do-ahead Mashed Potatoes

Servings: 6
Cooking Time: 50 Minutes

Ingredients:

- 5 Pound Yukon Gold or russet potatoes
- 9 Tablespoon butter
- 8 Ounce cream cheese
- 1/2 Cup milk
- salt and pepper

Directions:

1. Peel the potatoes and cut into chunks that are roughly the same size. Cover with cold water and add a teaspoon of salt. Bring to a boil over high heat, then reduce the heat to medium and simmer the potatoes until they are tender.
2. Drain the potatoes and return them to the pot. Stir over low heat for 2 to 3 minutes to evaporate any excess moisture.
3. Mash the potatoes with a hand-held potato masher. (Alternative, rice the potatoes using a ricer.) Incorporate 8 tbsp butter and cream cheese. Add milk until the potatoes are of a good consistency. Stir in salt and pepper to taste.
4. Butter the inside of a casserole dish. Spread the potatoes out in an even layer in the casserole dish, smoothing the top with a spatula. Cool, cover, and refrigerate if not cooking right away. Before cooking, let the potatoes warm to room temperature (about an hour).
5. Supply your smoker with wood pellets and follow the start-up procedure. Preheat the grill, with the lid closed, to 350° F.
6. Bake the potatoes for 45 to 50 minutes, or until hot through. Grill: 350 °F

Baked Stuffed Avocados

Servings: 6
Cooking Time: 15 Minutes

Ingredients:
- 4 avocados, halved and pit removed
- 8 eggs
- 2 Cup shredded cheddar cheese
- 1/4 Cup cherry tomatoes, halved
- 4 Slices Bacon, cooked & chopped
- salt and pepper
- 1 scallion, thinly sliced

Directions:
1. Supply your smoker with wood pellets and follow the start-up procedure. Preheat the grill, with the lid closed, to 450° F.
2. After removing the pit from the avocado, scoop out a little of the flesh to make enough room to fit 1 egg per half.
3. Fill the bottom of a cast iron pan with kosher salt and nestle the avocado halves into the salt, cut side up. The salt helps to keep them in place while cooking, like ice with oysters.
4. Crack one egg into each half, top with shredded cheddar cheese, cherry tomatoes and bacon. Season with salt and pepper to taste.
5. Place the cast iron pan directly on the grill grate and bake the avocados for 12 to 15 minutes until the cheese is melted and the egg is just set. Grill: 450 °F
6. Remove from the grill and let rest 5 to 10 minutes. Top with sliced scallions and enjoy!

Roasted Asparagus

Servings: 4
Cooking Time: 30 Minutes

Ingredients:
- 1 Bunch asparagus
- 2 Tablespoon olive oil, plus more as needed
- Veggie Rub

Directions:
1. Coat asparagus with olive oil and Veggie Rub, stirring to coat all pieces.
2. Supply your smoker with wood pellets and follow the start-up procedure. Preheat the grill, with the lid closed, to 350° F.
3. Place asparagus directly on the grill grate for 15-20 minutes.
4. Remove from grill and enjoy!

Butternut Squash

Servings: 4
Cooking Time: 45 Minutes

Ingredients:
- 1 Whole butternut squash
- Veggie Rub
- Blackened Saskatchewan Rub
- olive oil

Directions:
1. Cut squash in half and lightly coat with mixture of olive oil, Traeger Veggie Shake, and Traeger Blackened Saskatchewan.
2. Wrap in foil with 1/2 cup (120mL) of water.
3. Supply your smoker with wood pellets and follow the start-up procedure. Preheat the grill, with the lid closed, to 450° F.
4. Place squash on grill for 45 minutes. Remove from grill and unwrap. Enjoy!

Roasted Sweet Potato Steak Fries

Servings: 4
Cooking Time: 40 Minutes

Ingredients:

- 3 Whole sweet potatoes
- 4 Tablespoon extra-virgin olive oil
- salt and pepper
- 2 Tablespoon fresh chopped rosemary

Directions:

1. Supply your smoker with wood pellets and follow the start-up procedure. Preheat the grill, with the lid closed, to 450° F.
2. Cut sweet potatoes into wedges and toss with olive oil, salt, pepper and rosemary. Spread on a parchment lined baking sheet and put in the grill. Cook for 15 minutes then flip and continue to cook until lightly browned and cooked through, about 40 to 45 minutes total. Grill: 450 °F
3. Serve with your favorite dipping sauce. Enjoy! Grill: 450 °F

Grilled Asparagus And Spinach Salad

Servings: 8
Cooking Time: 10 Minutes

Ingredients:

- 4 Fluid Ounce apple cider vinegar
- 8 Fluid Ounce Honey Bourbon BBQ Sauce
- 2 Bunch asparagus, ends trimmed
- 3 Fluid Ounce extra-virgin olive oil
- 2 Ounce Beef Rub
- 24 Ounce Spinach, fresh
- 4 Ounce candied pecans
- 4 Ounce feta cheese

Directions:

1. Combine apple cider vinegar and Traeger Apricot BBQ Sauce to create salad dressing.
2. Supply your smoker with wood pellets and follow the start-up procedure. Preheat the grill, with the lid closed, to High heat.
3. Toss the asparagus with Olive Oil and the Beef Shake. Put asparagus in the Traeger Grilling Basket and move the basket to the grill grate.
4. Grill for about 10 minutes. Remove the asparagus once it is cooked. Grill: 350 °F
5. Place the hot asparagus right on top of the bowl of spinach.
6. Add candied pecans, feta cheese & salad dressing then toss and serve. Enjoy!

Grilled Broccoli Rabe

Servings: 4
Cooking Time: 10 Minutes

Ingredients:

- 4 Tablespoon extra-virgin olive oil
- 4 Bunch broccoli rabe or broccolini
- kosher salt
- 1 lemon, halved

Directions:

1. Supply your smoker with wood pellets and follow the start-up procedure. Preheat the grill, with the lid closed, to 450° F.
2. On a platter or in a mixing bowl, drizzle the olive oil over the broccoli rabe. Use your hands to mix thoroughly, coating the vegetables evenly with the oil. Season with sea salt.
3. Place the broccoli rabe in one layer directly on the lowest grill grate. Close the lid and cook for 5 to 10 minutes. You want there to be some color and slight char on the first side. Flip and cook for a few more minutes. Grill: 450 °F
4. Transfer the broccoli rabe to a serving platter and squeeze the juice of half a lemon evenly over the top.
5. Serve with more lemon wedges on the side. Enjoy!

Mashed Red Potatoes

Servings: 4
Cooking Time: 40 Minutes

Ingredients:
- 8 Large red potatoes
- salt
- black pepper
- 1/2 Cup heavy cream
- 1/4 Cup butter

Directions:
1. Supply your smoker with wood pellets and follow the start-up procedure. Preheat the grill, with the lid closed, to 180° F.
2. Slice red potatoes in half, lengthwise then cut in half again to make quarters. Season potatoes with salt and pepper.
3. Increase the heat to High and preheat. Once the grill is hot, set potatoes directly on the grill grate. Grill: 450 °F
4. Every 15 minutes flip potatoes to ensure all sides get color. Continue to do this until potatoes are fork tender.
5. When tender, mash potatoes with cream, butter, salt, and pepper to taste. Serve warm, enjoy!

Roasted Tomatoes With Hot Pepper Sauce

Servings: 4
Cooking Time: 60 Minutes

Ingredients:
- 2 Pound fresh Roma tomatoes
- 3 Tablespoon parsley, chopped
- 2 Tablespoon garlic, chopped
- salt and pepper
- 1/2 Cup extra-virgin olive oil
- 1 Pound Spaghetti
- Hot peppers

Directions:
1. Supply your smoker with wood pellets and follow the start-up procedure. Preheat the grill, with the lid closed, to 400° F.
2. Wash tomatoes and cut them in half, lengthwise. Place them in a baking dish cut side up.
3. Sprinkle with chopped parsley, garlic, add salt and black pepper and pour 1/4 cup (100 mL)of olive oil over them.
4. Place on pre-heated grill and bake for 1 1/2 hours. Tomatoes will shrink and the skins will be partly blackened. Grill: 400 °F
5. Remove tomatoes from baking dish and place in a food processor leaving the cooked oil, and puree them.
6. Drop pasta into boiling salted water and cook until tender. Drain and toss immediately with the pureed tomatoes.
7. Add the remaining 1/4 cup (60mL) of raw olive oil and crumbled hot red pepper to taste. Toss and serve. Enjoy!

Baked Artichoke Parmesan Mushrooms

Servings: 8
Cooking Time: 30 Minutes

Ingredients:
- 8 Cremini Mushroom Caps
- 6 1/2 Ounce artichoke hearts
- 1/3 Cup Parmesan cheese, grated
- 1/4 Cup mayonnaise
- 1/2 Teaspoon garlic salt
- your favorite hot sauce
- paprika

Directions:
1. Clean the mushrooms with a damp paper towel. Remove the stems and discard or save for another use.
2. Using a small spoon, scoop out the inside (gills, etc.). Combine the artichoke hearts, parmesan, mayonnaise, garlic salt, and hot sauce and mix well.
3. Mound the filling in the mushroom caps. Dust the tops with paprika.
4. Arrange the mushrooms in an oven-safe baking dish.
5. Supply your smoker with wood pellets and follow the start-up procedure. Preheat the grill, with the lid closed, to 350° F.
6. Bake the mushrooms (uncovered) until the filling is bubbling and just beginning to brown, about 25 to 30 minutes. Serve immediately. Grill: 350 °F
7. For a simple variation, stuff the mushrooms with your favorite bulk sausage and bake on your Traeger as directed above. Enjoy!

Smoked Beet-pickled Eggs

Servings: 4
Cooking Time: 30 Minutes

Ingredients:
- 6 Eggs, hard boiled
- 1 Red Beets, scrubbed and trimmed
- 1 Cup apple cider vinegar
- 1 Cup Beet, juice
- 1/4 Onion, Sliced
- 1/3 Cup granulated sugar
- 3 Cardamom
- 1 star anise

Directions:
1. Supply your smoker with wood pellets and follow the start-up procedure. Preheat the grill, with the lid closed, to 275° F.
2. Place the peeled hard boiled eggs directly on the grill and smoke for 30 minutes. Grill: 275 °F
3. Put the smoked eggs in a quart size glass jar with the cooked/chopped beets in the bottom.
4. In a medium sauce pan, add the vinegar, beet juice, onion, sugar, cardamom and anise.
5. Bring to a boil and cook, uncovered, until sugar has dissolved and the onions are translucent (about 5 minutes).
6. Remove from the heat and let cool for a few minutes.
7. Pour the vinegar and onions mixture over the eggs and beets in the jar, covering the eggs completely.
8. Securely close with the jar lid. Refrigerate up to a month. Enjoy!

Double-smoked Cheese Potatoes

Servings: 12
Cooking Time: 35 Minutes

Ingredients:
- 4 large baking potatoes (12 to 14 ounces each—preferably organic)
- 1 1/2 tablespoons bacon fat or butter, melted, or extra virgin olive oil
- Coarse salt (sea or kosher) and freshly ground black pepper
- 4 strips artisanal bacon (like Nueske's), cut crosswise into 1/4-inch slivers
- 6 tablespoons (3/4 stick) cold unsalted butter, thinly sliced
- 2 scallions, trimmed, white and green parts finely chopped (about 4 tablespoons)

- 2 cups coarsely grated smoked or regular white cheddar cheese (about 8 ounces)
- 1/2 cup sour cream
- Spanish smoked paprika (pimentón) or sweet paprika, for sprinkling

Directions:

1. Supply your smoker with wood pellets and follow the start-up procedure. Preheat the grill, with the lid closed, to 400° F. Add enough wood for 1 hour of smoking as specified by the manufacturer.
2. Scrub the potatoes on all sides with a vegetable brush. Rinse well under cold running water and blot dry with paper towels. Prick each potato several times with a fork (this keeps the spud from exploding and facilitates the smoke absorption). Brush or rub the potato on all sides with the bacon fat and season generously with salt and pepper.
3. Place the potatoes on the smoker rack. Smoke until the skins are crisp and the potatoes are tender in the center (they'll be easy to pierce with a slender metal skewer), about 1 hour.
4. Meanwhile, place the bacon in a cold skillet and fry over medium heat until browned and crisp, 3 to 4 minutes. Drain off the bacon fat (save the fat for future potatoes).
5. Transfer the potatoes to a cutting board and let cool slightly. Cut each potato in half lengthwise. Using a spoon, scrape out most of the potato flesh, leaving a 1/4-inch-thick shell. (It's easier to scoop the potatoes when warm.) Cut the potato flesh into 1/2-inch dice and place in a bowl.
6. Add the bacon, 4 tablespoons of the butter, the scallions, and cheese to the potato flesh and gently stir to mix. Stir in the sour cream and salt and pepper to taste; the mixture should be highly seasoned. Stir as little and as gently as possible so as to leave some texture to the potatoes.
7. Spoon the potato mixture back into the potato shells, mounding it in the center. Top each potato half with a thin slice of the remaining butter and sprinkle with paprika. The potatoes can be prepared up to 24 hours ahead to this stage covered, and refrigerated.
8. Just before serving, preheat your smoker to 400 °F. Add enough wood for 30 minutes of smoking. Place the potatoes in a shallow aluminum foil pan and re-smoke them until browned and bubbling, 15 to 20 minutes.

Roasted Fall Vegetables

Servings: 6
Cooking Time: 30 Minutes

Ingredients:

- 1/2 Pound Potatoes, new
- 2 Tablespoon olive oil
- salt and pepper
- 1/2 Pound Butternut Squash, diced
- 1/2 Pound fresh Brussels sprouts
- 1 Pint mushrooms, sliced

Directions:

1. Supply your smoker with wood pellets and follow the start-up procedure. Preheat the grill, with the lid closed, to 200° F.
2. Toss potatoes and squash with olive oil, salt and pepper and spread out on a sheet tray.
3. Place directly on the grill grate and cook for 15 minutes. Add brussels sprouts and mushrooms and toss to coat.
4. Cook another 15-20 minutes until veggies are lightly browned and cooked through.
5. Adjust seasoning as needed. Enjoy!

Roasted Red Pepper White Bean Dip

Servings: 4
Cooking Time: 40 Minutes

Ingredients:
- 4 Whole garlic
- 4 Tablespoon extra-virgin olive oil
- 2 Bell Pepper, Red
- 3 Tablespoon Dill Weed, fresh
- 3 Tablespoon chopped flat-leaf parsley
- 2 Can cannellini beans, mashed
- 4 Teaspoon lemon juice
- 1 1/2 Teaspoon salt

Directions:
1. Roasting the garlic and red peppers:
2. Supply your smoker with wood pellets and follow the start-up procedure. Preheat the grill, with the lid closed, to 400° F.
3. Peel away the outside layers of the garlic husk. Cut off the top of the garlic bulb, exposing each of the individual cloves. Drizzle olive oil over the top of the head of garlic and rub it in. Wrap the garlic in foil, completely covering it. Put the head of garlic and the two red peppers (washed and dried) on the Traeger.
4. Roast the garlic for 25-30 minutes and the peppers for about 40 minutes. Rotate the peppers a quarter-turn every 10 minutes until the exterior is blistered and blackened. Grill: 400 °F
5. Pull the peppers off the grill and put them in a bowl. Cover the bowl with plastic wrap and leave them for 15 minutes. The steam will loosen the skins so that they slip off like a drumstick covered in barbecue sauce.
6. Peel off the pepper skin. Cut off the stems and scrape out the seeds and they're ready to use.
7. As for the garlic, let it cool and then pull out the individual cloves as needed.
8. The dip:
9. In a blender put the roasted red peppers, 4 cloves of roasted garlic, dill, parsley, drained and rinsed beans, olive oil, lemon juice and salt.
10. Blend until the dip is smooth and creamy. You may need to scrape down the sides of the blender a couple of times. If it's having difficulty blending or looks too thick add more olive oil or lemon juice. (Add more lemon juice if it tastes like it needs more acid or brightness.) Enjoy!

Grilled Street Corn

Servings: 6
Cooking Time: 10 Minutes

Ingredients:
- 6 ears corn, husked
- 1 As Needed extra-virgin olive oil
- 1/4 Cup mayonnaise
- 1 Tablespoon ancho or guajillo chile powder
- 1/2 Cup chopped cilantro, plus more for serving
- 1 lime, zested and juiced
- salt
- 1/2 Cup Cotija cheese
- 1 As Needed cilantro, finely chopped

Directions:
1. Supply your smoker with wood pellets and follow the start-up procedure. Preheat the grill, with the lid closed, to 450° F.
2. Brush corn with oil and place on grill, turning occasionally.
3. While corn is on the grill, mix mayonnaise with chile powder, cilantro, lime juice and zest in a bowl. Season with salt.

4. After about 10 minutes corn should be cooked through and slightly charred on the outside. Remove from grill.

5. Top corn with chile mayonnaise then sprinkle on the Cotija cheese and chopped cilantro. Enjoy!

Green Bean Casserole

Servings: 6
Cooking Time: 25 Minutes

Ingredients:
- 1/2 Stick butter
- 1 Small onion
- 1/2 Cup sliced button mushrooms
- 4 Can green beans, drained
- 2 Can cream of mushroom soup
- 1 Teaspoon Lawry's Seasoned Salt
- pepper
- 1 Can French's Original Crispy Fried Onions
- 1 Cup grated sharp cheddar cheese

Directions:
1. Supply your smoker with wood pellets and follow the start-up procedure. Preheat the grill, with the lid closed, to 375° F.
2. Melt butter in a cast iron skillet and add onions and mushrooms, stirring occasionally until softened.
3. Add drained green beans and cream of mushroom soup and stir gently to combine.
4. Season with seasoned salt and pepper and sprinkle the top with grated cheddar cheese and fried onions.
5. Bake for 25 minutes. Serve warm, enjoy! Grill: 375 °F

Grilled Asparagus & Honey-glazed Carrots

Servings: 4
Cooking Time: 35 Minutes

Ingredients:
- 1 Bunch asparagus, woody ends removed
- 1 Pound Carrots, peeled
- 2 Tablespoon olive oil
- sea salt
- 2 Tablespoon honey
- lemon zest

Directions:
1. Rinse all vegetables under cold water. Drizzle asparagus with olive oil and a generous sprinkling of sea salt. Generously drizzle carrots with honey and lightly sprinkle with sea salt.
2. Supply your smoker with wood pellets and follow the start-up procedure. Preheat the grill, with the lid closed, to 350° F.
3. Place carrots on the grill first and cook for 10-15 minutes, then add asparagus and cook both for another 15 to 20 minutes, or until they're done to your liking. Grill: 350 °F
4. Top the asparagus with some fresh lemon zest Enjoy!

Roasted New Potatoes With Compound Butter

Servings: 4
Cooking Time: 45 Minutes

Ingredients:
- 2 Pound Small Red, White or Purple Potatoes (or Combination of All Three)
- 3 Tablespoon olive oil
- salt and pepper
- 2 Stick Butter, unsalted
- 1 Tablespoon shallot, minced
- 3 Tablespoon Finely Chopped Herbs, Such As Tarragon, Parsley, Basil or Combination

- 2 Teaspoon kosher salt

Directions:

1. Supply your smoker with wood pellets and follow the start-up procedure. Preheat the grill, with the lid closed, to 400° F. Cut the potatoes in half and place in a large mixing bowl. Cover with the olive oil, a teaspoon of salt and generous grinding of pepper.
2. Place on a large baking sheet so there is space between the potatoes. Place on the grill and roast for 45 minutes to 1 hour, until crispy skinned. Toss once during cooking. Grill: 400 °F
3. To make the butter: Place it in a medium sized shallow mixing bowl. Use a wooden spoon or strong spatula to break it up and soften it even more. Sprinkle the shallot, herbs, and salt over the butter, then use the spoon to combine the ingredients. Taste, adding more salt or herbs if necessary. Reserve a few tablespoons of the butter to serve on the potatoes.
4. To freeze the butter for future use, place a foot long piece of plastic wrap on the counter. Spread the butter out into a 6" log across the long direction of the plastic wrap towards the bottom. Begin to roll the plastic wrap away from you to roll it into a log, twisting the sides of the plastic wrap like a candy wrapper to secure.
5. Using your hands, shape the log into an even cylinder. Once it's wrapped tightly, place in the freezer. Then when more is needed, simply slice off coins of it to serve over grilled steak, chicken, veggies, or roasted potatoes. The butter holds well in the freezer for up to one month. Enjoy!
*Cook times will vary depending on set and ambient temperatures.

Sicilian Stuffed Mushrooms

Servings: 6
Cooking Time: 25 Minutes

Ingredients:

- 12 Medium Fresh Mushrooms, about 1-1/2 inches in diameter
- 4 Ounce cream cheese, room temperature
- 1/4 Cup Parmesan cheese, grated
- 1/4 Cup shredded mozzarella cheese
- 8 Whole Pimento Stuffed Green Olives, chopped
- 3 Tablespoon Pepperoni, finely diced
- 1 1/2 Tablespoon Sun Dried Tomatoes, drained & minced
- 1/4 Teaspoon freshly ground black pepper

Directions:

1. Dampen a paper towel and wipe the outside of the mushrooms clean. Remove the stem. Using a small spoon, scoop out the inside of the mushroom leaving a shell.
2. Filling: In a small mixing bowl, beat together the cream cheese, Parmesan, and mozzarella. Stir in olives, pepperoni, tomatoes, basil, and pepper.
3. Mound the filling in the mushroom caps. Set each filled cap into the well of a muffin tin.
4. Supply your smoker with wood pellets and follow the start-up procedure. Preheat the grill, with the lid closed, to 350° F.
5. Arrange the muffin tin on the grill grate and bake the mushrooms for 25 to 30 minutes, or until the mushrooms are tender and the filling is beginning to brown.
6. Transfer to a serving plate or platter. Enjoy!

Smoked Mushrooms

Servings: 4
Cooking Time: 45 Minutes

Ingredients:
- Pound Mushrooms, fresh
- 1/2 Cup apple cider vinegar
- 1/2 Cup soy sauce
- 1 Teaspoon Blackened Saskatchewan Rub

Directions:
1. Clean mushrooms and place in a large Ziploc bag. Add apple cider vinegar, soy sauce and rub.
2. Mix well and allow to marinate in the refrigerator for at least 2 hours.
3. Supply your smoker with wood pellets and follow the start-up procedure. Preheat the grill, with the lid closed, to 350° F.
4. Place cast iron skillet inside grill for 20 minutes to warm up.
5. Add the mushrooms and marinade slowly into the cast iron skillet.
6. Cook uncovered for 15 minutes, then cover the skillet and cook another 30 minutes until mushrooms are tender. Grill: 350 °F
7. Remove skillet from grill and let mushrooms cool down for 5 minutes before serving. Enjoy!

Smoked & Loaded Baked Potato

Servings: 4
Cooking Time: 60 Minutes

Ingredients:
- 6 Yukon Gold or russet potatoes
- 8 Slices bacon
- 1/2 Cup butter, melted
- 1 Cup sour cream
- 1 1/2 Cup shredded cheddar cheese, divided
- salt and pepper
- 1 Bunch green onions, thinly sliced

Directions:
1. Supply your smoker with wood pellets and follow the start-up procedure. Preheat the grill, with the lid closed, to 375° F.
2. Poke potatoes with a fork, then place straight onto the grill. Cook for 1 hour. Grill: 375 °F
3. At the same time, cook bacon on a baking sheet on the grill for about 20 minutes; remove, cool and crumble. Grill: 375 °F
4. Once potatoes are done, remove and allow to cool for 15 minutes.
5. Cut each potato lengthwise, creating long halves. Use a small spoon to scoop out about 70% of the potato to make a boat, keeping a thick layer of potato near skin.
6. Place excess potato in a bowl and reserve. Lightly mash extra potato with a fork; add butter, sour cream, 1/2 cup cheese and season with salt and pepper.
7. Take the potato skins and fill with potato mixture, then sprinkle with extra cheese and bacon.
8. Place back on grill for about 10 minutes or until warm and cheese has melted. Garnish with green onions and extra sour cream. Enjoy! Grill: 375 °F

Grilled Corn On The Cob With Parmesan And Garlic

Servings: 6
Cooking Time: 30 Minutes

Ingredients:
- 4 Tablespoon butter, melted
- 2 Clove garlic, minced
- salt and pepper
- 8 ears fresh corn

- 1/2 Cup shaved Parmesan
- 1 Tablespoon chopped parsley

Directions:
1. Supply your smoker with wood pellets and follow the start-up procedure. Preheat the grill, with the lid closed, to 450° F.
2. Place butter, garlic, salt and pepper in a medium bowl and mix well.
3. Peel back corn husks and remove the silk. Rub corn with half of the garlic butter mixture.
4. Close husks and place directly on the grill grate. Cook for 25 to 30 minutes, turning occasionally until corn is tender. Grill: 450 °F
5. Remove from grill, peel and discard husks. Place corn on serving tray, drizzle with remaining butter and top with Parmesan and parsley.

Tater Tot Bake

Servings: 4
Cooking Time: 15 Minutes

Ingredients:
- 1 Whole frozen tater tots
- salt and pepper
- 1 Cup sour cream
- 1 Cup shredded cheddar cheese, divided
- 1/2 Cup bacon, chopped
- 1/4 Cup green onion, diced

Directions:
1. Supply your smoker with wood pellets and follow the start-up procedure. Preheat the grill, with the lid closed, to 375° F.
2. Line a baking sheet with aluminum foil for easy clean up and spread frozen tater tots onto sheet.
3. Sprinkle with Veggie Shake or salt and pepper to taste.
4. Place the baking sheet on the preheated grill grate and cook the tater tots for 10 minutes.
5. Drizzle sour cream over cooked tater tots.
6. Sprinkle the cheese, bacon bits and green onions on top of the tater tots.
7. Turn heat up to High heat and cook for 5 more minutes until the cheese melts and serve immediately. Enjoy!

Skillet Potato Cake

Servings: 4
Cooking Time: 40 Minutes

Ingredients:
- 8 Tablespoon butter, melted
- 2 Pound russet potatoes, peeled and thinly sliced
- 3 Tablespoon kosher salt
- 2 Tablespoon freshly ground black pepper
- thyme

Directions:
1. Supply your smoker with wood pellets and follow the start-up procedure. Preheat the grill, with the lid closed, to 375° F.
2. Brush the bottom of a cast iron skillet with part of the melted butter. Place potato slices vertically around the outer edges then fill in the middle in the same fashion.
3. Pour additional melted butter over the top of the layers and sprinkle with salt and pepper.
4. Place skillet in grill and cook for 35 to 40 minutes or until potatoes are fork tender and golden brown.
5. Garnish with a sprinkle of fresh thyme over the top of the potatoes. Enjoy!

Baked Breakfast Mini Quiches

Servings: 8
Cooking Time: 15 Minutes

Ingredients:
- cooking spray
- 1 Tablespoon extra-virgin olive oil
- 1/2 yellow onion, diced
- 3 Cup Spinach, fresh
- 10 eggs
- 4 Ounce shredded cheddar, mozzarella or Swiss cheese
- 1/4 Cup fresh basil
- 1 Teaspoon kosher salt
- 1/2 Teaspoon black pepper

Directions:

1. Spray a 12-cup muffin tin generously with cooking spray.
2. In a small skillet over medium heat, warm the oil. Add the onion and cook, stirring frequently, until softened, about 7 minutes. Add the spinach and cook until wilted, about 1 minute longer.
3. Transfer to a cutting board to cool, then chop the mixture so the spinach if broken up a little.
4. Supply your smoker with wood pellets and follow the start-up procedure. Preheat the grill, with the lid closed, to 350° F.
5. In a large bowl, whisk the eggs until frothy. Add the cooled onions and spinach, cheese, basil, 1 tsp salt and 1/2 tsp pepper. Stir to combine. Divide egg mixture evenly among the muffin cups.
6. Place tray on the grill and bake until the eggs have puffed up, are set, and are beginning to brown, about 18 to 20 minutes. Grill: 350 °F
7. Serve immediately, or allow to cool on a wire rack, then refrigerate in an air tight container for up to 4 days. Enjoy!

POULTRY RECIPES

Spiced Bbq Turkey

Servings: 8
Cooking Time: 120 Minutes

Ingredients:
- 1 Bay Leaf
- 1/2 Tsp Black Peppercorns, Ground
- Pinch Chili Flakes
- 4 Garlic Cloves, Peeled And Smashed
- 1/4 Cup Honey
- 3/4 Cup Honey Chipotle Bbq Sauce
- 1 Honeysuckle White® Turkey, Thawed
- 1 Tsp Kosher Salt
- 1/4 Cup Olive Oil
- 3 Thyme Sprigs
- 1 Cup Turkey Stock
- 3 Cups Water
- 2 Tbsp Worcestershire Sauce

Directions:
1. Rinse Honeysuckle White® turkey thoroughly under cold water, then blot dry with paper towels. Place on a greased rack of a roasting pan. Set aside.
2. Prepare the injection solution: in a saucepot, whisk together the turkey stock, honey, olive oil, smashed garlic, Worcestershire sauce, salt, pepper, and chili flakes. Add in the thyme sprigs and bay leaf. Bring mixture to a boil, then simmer for 5 minutes. Remove from heat, cool for 30 minutes, then strain.
3. Using an injection needle, inject the solution throughout the turkey. Rub 1 tablespoon of solution over the top of the turkey. Add water to the bottom of the roasting pan. Set aside.
4. Supply your smoker with wood pellets and follow the start-up procedure. Preheat the grill, with the lid closed, to 450° F. If using a gas or charcoal grill, set it up for high heat.
5. Transfer the turkey to the grill and roast for 100 to 120 minutes, until an internal temperature of 165° F is reached, rotating every 30 minutes. Tent with foil after 30 minutes, then brush all over with BBQ sauce during the final 10 minutes of roasting time.
6. Remove from the grill, and allow the turkey to rest for 30 minutes, then carve and serve warm.

Chicken Breast Calzones

Servings: 4
Cooking Time: 24 Minutes

Ingredients:
- 4 boneless, skinless chicken breasts, each about 6 to 8oz (170 to 225g)
- coarse salt
- freshly ground black pepper
- 1 cup good-quality Italian tomato sauce or marinara
- 4oz (110g) thinly sliced pepperoni or diced smoked ham
- 4oz (110g) provolone, fontina, or mozzarella cheese
- 8 fresh basil leaves
- 4 thin slices of prosciutto
- extra virgin olive oil
- freshly grated Parmesan cheese

Directions:
1. Supply your smoker with wood pellets and follow the start-up procedure. Preheat the grill, with the lid closed, to 425° F.

2. Use a sharp, thin-bladed knife to cut a deep pocket in the side of each breast, angling the knife toward the opposite side. (Don't cut all the way through.) Season the inside of each breast with salt and pepper. Add a couple spoonfuls of tomato sauce to each pocket. Add 1 ounce (25g) of pepperoni, 1 ounce (25g) of provolone, and 2 basil leaves.

3. Wrap each breast crosswise with a slice of prosciutto and then pin each breast closed with two toothpicks. Lightly brush the breasts with olive oil and season the outside with salt and pepper.

4. Place the breasts on the grate at an angle to the bars. Grill for 10 to 12 minutes and then turn with a thin-bladed spatula. Dust the tops with grated Parmesan. Continue to cook until the chicken is cooked through and the cheese has melted, about 10 to 12 minutes more.

5. Transfer the chicken to a platter. Let rest for 3 minutes and then remove the toothpicks. Serve immediately.

Beer Chicken

Servings: 4
Cooking Time: 75 Minutes

Ingredients:
- 1 Beer, Can
- 1 Chicken, Whole
- Lemon Pepper Garlic Seasoning

Directions:
1. Supply your smoker with wood pellets and follow the start-up procedure. Preheat the grill, with the lid open, to 400° F.
2. Season the chicken all over with spices. Open the can of your favorite pop/beer and place the opening of the chicken over the can. Make sure that the chicken can stand upright without falling over. Place on your Grill and barbecue until the internal temperature reaching 165 degrees F (about an hour).
3. Remove from grill, slice and serve hot.

Cajun Brined Maple Smoked Turkey Breast

Servings: 4
Cooking Time: 180 Minutes

Ingredients:
- 1 Gallon water
- 3/4 Cup canning and pickling salt
- 3 Tablespoon minced garlic
- 3 Tablespoon dark brown sugar
- 2 Tablespoon Worcestershire sauce
- 2 Tablespoon Cajun seasoning
- 1 (5-6 lb) bone-in turkey breast
- 3 Tablespoon extra-virgin olive oil
- 2 Tablespoon Cajun seasoning

Directions:
1. In a large food safe container or bucket, combine all of the ingredients for the brine with 1 gallon water. Stir until the salt is dissolved.
2. Place the turkey breast in the brine and weigh it down to ensure it is fully submerged. Cover and brine in a refrigerator for 1 to 2 days.
3. Remove the turkey breast from the brine and pat dry. Drizzle with the olive oil using your hands to cover all areas of the bird. Season liberally with Cajun seasoning. Probe: 165 °F
4. Supply your smoker with wood pellets and follow the start-up procedure. Preheat the grill, with the lid closed, to 225° F.
5. Place the turkey breast directly on the grill grate, close the lid and cook for 3 hours. After 3 hours, increase the temperature to 425°F and

continue to cook for another 30 minutes or until the internal temperature reads 165°F when a thermometer is inserted into the thickest part of the breast. Grill: 225 °F Probe: 165 °F

6. Remove the turkey breast from the grill and allow to rest for at least 15 minutes before slicing. Slice and serve. Enjoy!

Roasted Honey Bourbon Glazed Turkey

Servings: 8
Cooking Time: 240 Minutes

Ingredients:
- 1 Whole (18-20 lb) turkey
- 1/4 Cup Fin & Feather Rub
- 1/2 Cup bourbon
- 1/2 Cup honey
- 1/4 Cup brown sugar
- 3 Tablespoon apple cider vinegar
- 1 Tablespoon Dijon mustard
- salt and pepper

Directions:
1. Supply your smoker with wood pellets and follow the start-up procedure. Preheat the grill, with the lid closed, to 375° F. Truss the turkey legs together. Season the exterior of the bird and the cavity with Traeger Fin and Feather Rub.
2. Place the turkey directly on the grill grate and cook for 20-30 minutes at 375°F or until the skin begins to brown. Grill: 375 °F
3. After 30 minutes, reduce the temperature to 325°F and continue to cook until internal temperature registers 165°F when an instant read thermometer is inserted into the thickest part of the breast, about 3-4 hours. Grill: 325 °F Probe: 165 °F
4. For the Whiskey Glaze: Combine all ingredients in a small saucepan and bring to a boil. Reduce the temperature and let simmer 15-20 minutes or until thick enough to coat the back of a spoon. Remove from heat and set aside.
5. During the last ten minutes of cooking, brush the glaze on the turkey while on the grill and cook until the glaze is set, about 10 minutes. Remove from grill and let rest 10-15 minutes before carving. Enjoy! *Cook times will vary depending on set and ambient temperatures.

Delicious Smoked Turketta

Servings: 6
Cooking Time: 180 Minutes

Ingredients:
- 1 Shady Brook Farms® Turketta

Directions:
1. Supply your smoker with wood pellets and follow the start-up procedure. Preheat the grill, with the lid closed, to 250° F. If using a gas or charcoal grill, set it up for low, indirect heat.
2. Place the Turketta directly on the grill grate and smoke for 2½ to 3 hours, or until an internal temperature of 165°F is reached.

Glazed Bbq Half Chicken

Servings: 6
Cooking Time: 120 Minutes

Ingredients:
- Meat Church Bird Bath Poultry Brine
- 1/2 Gallon water or chicken stock
- 1 Whole chicken
- 1 Whole whole chicken
- Meat Church Holy Gospel BBQ Rub
- 1 Stick butter
- Cup favorite BBQ sauce

- 2 Teaspoon blackberry jelly, pepper jelly or your favorite jelly

Directions:

1. Mix the Meat Church Bird Bath Poultry Brine thoroughly in a 1/2 gallon of water or chicken stock. Feel free to be creative and add ingredients to enhance the flavor profile to your liking. Completely submerge the chicken in the brine mixture and place in the refrigerator overnight. We recommend 12 to 24 hours for this brine.

2. Remove the bird from the brine. Rinse off and pat dry with a paper towel.

3. Supply your smoker with wood pellets and follow the start-up procedure. Preheat the grill, with the lid closed, to 275° F.

4. Using a pair of chicken shears or a very sharp knife, remove the backbone. Do this by trimming along one side of the backbone from one end of the chicken to the other. Then repeat the process on the other side of the backbone and remove it completely. Open the chicken once the backbone is removed. At this point you can remove the breastbone if you like. Slice the bird in half using a sharp knife. Now you have 2 half chickens.

5. Apply Meat Church Holy Gospel BBQ Rub to all sides of the chicken; underneath and on top of the skin. We also recommend working your hands underneath the chicken skin and applying rub directly on the meat. This will ensure a really flavorful bite even if they don't get any skin.

6. Place the chicken halves and butter in a half steam pan and put the pan on the Traeger. Baste the chicken with the butter periodically throughout the cook.

7. Using an instant-read thermometer, remove the chicken from the grill when they reach an internal temperature of at least 165°F in the deepest part of the breast, about 1-1/2 to 2 hours. Grill: 275 °F Probe: 165 °F

8. For the glaze, mix the BBQ sauce, honey and jelly and heat in a small sauce pan.

Bbq Spatchcocked Chicken

Servings: 2
Cooking Time: 45 Minutes

Ingredients:

- 1 whole chicken
- 1/4 Cup Chicken Rub
- olive oil
- 1/2 Cup Sweet & Heat BBQ Sauce

Directions:

1. Supply your smoker with wood pellets and follow the start-up procedure. Preheat the grill, with the lid closed, to 375° F.

2. With a large knife or shears, cut the bird open along the backbone on both sides, through the ribs, and remove the backbone.

3. Brush chicken with olive oil and season both sides with Traeger Chicken rub.

4. Place the poultry on the Traeger, breast side up and cook for 35 to 40 minutes or until a thermometer inserted into the breast registers 160°F. Grill: 375 °F Probe: 160 °F

5. Remove from the grill and let rest 5 minutes before slicing. Enjoy!

Italian Grilled Barbecue Chicken Wings

Servings: 4
Cooking Time: 18 Minutes

Ingredients:

- 1 cup KRAFT Zesty Italian Dressing

- 2 pounds chicken wings/drummettes
- 1/2 cup barbecue sauce

Directions:
1. Pour dressing over chicken in large bowl; toss to coat.
2. Refrigerate at least 30 minutes to marinate.
3. Supply your smoker with wood pellets and follow the start-up procedure. Preheat the grill, with the lid closed, to 400° F. Drain chicken; discard marinade.
4. Grill chicken 8 minutes on each side or until done.
5. Brush with barbecue sauce; grill for another 2 minutes.
6. Remove from grill and serve.

Bbq Cheese Chicken Stuffed Bell Peppers

Servings: 4
Cooking Time: 15 Minutes

Ingredients:
- ½ Cup Barbecue Sauce
- 4 Bell Pepper
- ½ Cup Cheddar Cheese, Shredded
- 2 Cups Leftover Chicken, Chopped
- 2 Tablespoons Champion Chicken Seasoning

Directions:
1. Wash and slice the bell peppers in half, longways. Deseed them and set aside.
2. Supply your smoker with wood pellets and follow the start-up procedure. Preheat the grill, with the lid open, to 350° F.
3. In a large bowl, mix together the cheese, chicken, Champion Chicken Seasoning, and barbecue sauce, then stuff inside the pepper halves.
4. Grill the peppers for 7-10 minutes or until the peppers are softened and the filling is heated through and melted. Remove from the grill and serve.

Fig Glazed Chicken Stuffed Cornbread

Servings: 10
Cooking Time: 120 Minutes

Ingredients:
- Black Pepper
- 6 Tablespoons (For The Chicken) Butter, Unsalted
- 3 Chicken, Whole
- 2 1/5 Cups (Replace With Craisins For A Different Flavor) Dried Figs, Chopped
- 1 Egg
- 2 Tablespoon Extra-Virgin Olive Oil
- 1/2 Cup Heavy Cream
- 1/2 Cup Honey
- Kosher Salt
- 4 Tablespoon Lemon, Juice
- 1/2 Onion, Chopped
- Champion Chicken Seasoning
- 1 1/2 Teaspoon Finely Chopped Rosemary, Fresh
- 1 Pound Sweet Italian Sausage
- 3 Cups Water, Warm

Directions:
1. Mix figs, honey, lemon juice, and warm water. Cover with plastic wrap and let figs soften for 30 minutes. Strain the figs and reserve the liquid for glaze.
2. Heat olive oil over medium heat and sauté the onions with rosemary. Add the sausage. Cook until browned. Place into a large bowl, add the cornbread and figs. Season with Champion

Chicken Seasoning. Stir. In a separate bowl, Stir together egg, heavy whipping cream, and chicken stock. Pour over the cornbread/fig mix and stir together. Set aside.

3. Rinse chickens and pat dry. Season liberally with Champion Chicken Seasoning, kosher salt and black pepper. Don't forget the cavity! Stuff cavities with Stuffing. Top each Chicken with 2 tablespoons butter.

4. Supply your smoker with wood pellets and follow the start-up procedure. Preheat the grill, with the lid closed, to 300° F. Place in a roasting tray and cook until internal temp reads 165°F.

5. While chickens cook, place the fig liquid, balsamic vinegar and butter over. Reduce to thicken and baste chickens with about 160°F or 10 minutes before finished. Rest for 10 minutes. Carve and serve!

Smoked Buffalo Fries

Servings: 4
Cooking Time: 30 Minutes

Ingredients:
- 4 Chicken Breast
- salt
- black pepper
- 2 Cup Blue Cheese Dressing
- 1/2 Cup Frank's RedHot Sauce
- 1 Celery, stalks
- 6 russet potatoes
- Oil, For Frying

Directions:

1. Supply your smoker with wood pellets and follow the start-up procedure. Preheat the grill, with the lid closed, to 325° F.

2. Season chicken breast with salt and pepper. Smoke for 25-30 minutes or until 165 degrees. Pull and set aside.

3. Whisk blue cheese dressing and hot sauce together in a bowl; set aside.

4. Soak cut celery (2" long sticks) in cold water until serving

5. Cut potatoes into ¼ in sticks, resembling French fries.

6. Heat oil to 375 degrees in a Dutch oven or deep pot and gently place in potatoes. Fry until golden brown, drain on a sheet pan lined with paper towels. Season with kosher or sea salt. Repeat until all the potatoes are cooked. Keep them warm in an oven until you are ready to serve

7. To assemble, place fries on a platter or wood board lined with butchers paper. Drizzle with franks sauce mixture, then the pulled chicken. Garnish with celery and serve immediately. Enjoy

Bbq Chicken Tostada

Servings: 4
Cooking Time: 50 Minutes

Ingredients:
- 4 Whole boneless, skinless chicken thighs
- salt and pepper
- 8 Whole Corn Tostada
- Refried Beans
- lettuce
- green onion, coarsely chopped
- cilantro, chopped
- guacamole

Directions:

1. Supply your smoker with wood pellets and follow the start-up procedure. Preheat the grill, with the lid closed, to 350° F.

2. While grill heats, trim excess fat and skin from chicken thighs.

3. Season with a light layer of salt and pepper.

4. Place chicken thighs on the grill grate and cook for 35 minutes.

5. Check internal temperature; chicken is done when a thermometer inserted reads 175 degrees F. Remove from the grill and let rest for 10 minutes before shredding.

6. Place tostadas on grill while chicken is resting for 5 minutes.

7. Build tostadas starting with refried beans, sliced lettuce, shredded chicken, tomatoes, green onions, cilantro, guacamole. Enjoy!

Smoked Cheesy Chicken Quesadilla

Servings: 4-8
Cooking Time: 180 Minutes

Ingredients:
- 2-3 Boneless, Skinless Chicken Breasts
- 1 Jalapeno, Chopped
- 1 Onion, Chopped
- Sweet Heat Rub
- 1, Chopped Red Bell Pepper
- 1-2 Cups Salsa
- 3 Cups Shredded Cheddar Cheese
- 3 Cups Shredded Monterey Or Pepper Jack Cheese
- Taco Sauce
- 20 Taco-Size Tortilla

Directions:

1. Supply your smoker with wood pellets and follow the start-up procedure. Preheat the grill, with the lid closed, to 350° F. If you're using a gas or charcoal grill, set it up for medium heat. Preheat with lid closed for 10-15 minutes.

2. Sprinkle chicken breasts generously in Sweet Heat Rub and rub to coat evenly. Place chicken breasts directly on preheated grill grates and cook for 45 minutes, or until the chicken is completely cooked (165°F internal temperature), tender, and falling apart. Remove from the grill and let cool slightly. Shred with meat claws and set aside. Turn grill up to 375°F.

3. In a large bowl, add the shredded chicken, onion, red bell pepper, jalapeno, and taco sauce. Mix to combine then set aside.

4. Cut each tortilla in half. Add about 2 tablespoons each of the cheddar cheese, Monterey Jack cheese, and chicken mixture to each tortilla half. Roll the tortillas into cones, starting from the cut edge, making sure not to push the ingredients out of the tortilla.

5. Place the small bowl in the center of the pizza plan and begin to stack quesadilla cones in a ring around the bowl. The points of each cone should be in the center just touching the bowl. Sprinkle cheese over the layer and repeat another layer with the remaining cones, finishing with a final sprinkle of cheese.

6. Remove bowl from the center of the ring and place the pizza pan directly on the grill grates. Cook with the lid closed for 15-20 minutes, or until the cheese is melted and the edges are browned and crispy.

7. Fill small bowl with salsa and return to the center of the ring. Serve immediately and enjoy!

Teriyaki Apple Cider Turkey

Servings: 8-10
Cooking Time: 180 Minutes

Ingredients:
- 1/2 Cup Apple Cider
- 1/4 Cup Melted Butter, Unsalted
- 1 Teaspoon Cornstarch
- 2 Finely Chopped Garlic, Cloves
- 1/2 Teaspoon Ginger, Ground
- 2 Tablespoon Honey
- 2 Tablespoon Champion Chicken Seasoning
- 1 Shady Brook Farms® Whole Turkey, Thawed
- 2 Tablespoon Soy Sauce
- 1 Tablespoon Water, Cold

Directions:
1. Supply your smoker with wood pellets and follow the start-up procedure. Preheat the grill, with the lid closed, to 300° F.
2. In a saucepan, whisk together melted butter, garlic, soy sauce, apple cider, ground ginger, and honey. Bring to a boil then reduce to a simmer.
3. Place the turkey in an aluminum roasting pan.
4. With a marinade injector, fill with the mixture and pierce the meat with the needle while pushing on the plunger, injecting the flavor. You want to inject into the thickest part of the breast, thigh, and wings.
5. Next, rub entire turkey with your favorite poultry seasoning or the Champion Chicken seasoning. For added flavor, throw some extra garlic gloves into the cavity and apple cider in the aluminum pan.
6. Place the turkey in the grill and cook until the internal temperature reaches 165-170°F.
7. In a separate bowl, mix cornstarch and cold water together and add to the leftover original mixture to create a glaze. Glaze the turkey with the remaining mixture with approximately 15-20 minutes left. Skin will darken because of the sugar in the glaze.
8. Let the turkey rest 20-25 minutes before carving and enjoy!

Smoked Whole Chicken

Servings: 6-8
Cooking Time: 240 Minutes

Ingredients:
- 1 whole chicken
- 2 cups Tea Injectable (using Not-Just-for-Pork Rub)
- 2 tablespoons olive oil
- 1 batch Chicken Rub
- 2 tablespoons butter, melted

Directions:
1. Supply your smoker with wood pellets and follow the start-up procedure. Preheat the grill, with the lid closed, to 180°F.
2. Inject the chicken throughout with the tea injectable.
3. Coat the chicken all over with olive oil and season it with the rub. Using your hands, work the rub into the meat.
4. Place the chicken directly on the grill grate and smoke for 3 hours.
5. Baste the chicken with the butter and increase the grill's temperature to 375°F. Continue to cook the chicken until its internal temperature reaches 170°F.
6. Remove the chicken from the grill and let it rest for 10 minutes, before carving and serving.

Oktoberfest Pretzel Mustard Chicken

Servings: 4
Cooking Time: 25 Minutes

Ingredients:
- 1/4 Pound pretzel sticks
- 3 Tablespoon Dijon mustard
- 3 Tablespoon apple cider or brown ale
- 1 Tablespoon honey
- 1 1/2 Teaspoon fresh thyme, plus more for garnish
- 4 boneless, skinless chicken breasts

Directions:
1. Pulse the pretzel sticks in a food processor or crush by hand in a resealable bag until they've turned into a powder the texture of panko breadcrumbs.
2. Transfer the crumbs to a wide, shallow bowl.
3. In separate shallow bowl, whisk mustard, beer or cider, honey and thyme together.
4. Spray a wire rack with cooking spray and place atop a sheet tray. Dip each chicken breast in the mustard mixture, then dredge in the pretzel crumbs to coat evenly and place on the wire rack. Spray the top of each chicken breast lightly with cooking spray.
5. Supply your smoker with wood pellets and follow the start-up procedure. Preheat the grill, with the lid closed, to 375° F.
6. Place the pan on the Traeger and bake for about 20 to 25 minutes, until the chicken breasts are fully cooked and register 165°F on an instant-read thermometer. Grill: 375 °F Probe: 165 °F
7. Let chicken rest for 5 minutes. Garnish with fresh thyme if desired. Enjoy!

Grilled Beantown Chicken Wings

Servings: 8
Cooking Time: 50 Minutes

Ingredients:
- 3 Pound chicken wings
- 1/4 Cup vegetable oil
- 1 1/2 Tablespoon Pork & Poultry Rub
- 1 Cup Irish Stout
- 1/2 Cup butter
- 2 Tablespoon apple jelly
- 1 Cup Frank's RedHot Sauce

Directions:
1. Rinse the chicken wings under cold running water and pat dry. With a sharp knife, cut the wings into three pieces through the joints. Discard the wing tips, or save for chicken stock.
2. Transfer the remaining "drumettes" and "flats" to a large a bowl. Add the oil and the Traeger Pork and Poultry shake, and toss with your hands to coat the wings evenly.
3. Make the beer sauce: In a small saucepan, bring the beer to a boil over high heat and reduce by half. Reduce the heat to medium-low and add the butter, stirring until melted. Stir in the apple jelly and the hot sauce. Keep warm.
4. Supply your smoker with wood pellets and follow the start-up procedure. Preheat the grill, with the lid closed, to 350° F.
5. Arrange the wings on the grill grate. Cook for 45 to 50 minutes, or until the chicken is no longer pink at the bone, turning once halfway through. Transfer the wings to a large clean bowl and pour the beer sauce over the wings, tossing to coat. Serve immediately. Grill: 350 °F

Smoked Wings

Servings: 6
Cooking Time: 50 Minutes

Ingredients:
- 24 chicken wings, flats and drumettes separated
- 12 Ounce Italian dressing
- 3 Ounce Chicken Rub
- 5 Ounce 'Que BBQ Sauce
- 3 Ounce chili sauce

Directions:
1. Wash all wings and place into resealable bag. Add Italian dressing to the resealable bag containing the wings. Place in refrigerator and allow to marinate for 6 to 12 hours.
2. Supply your smoker with wood pellets and follow the start-up procedure. Preheat the grill, with the lid closed, to 225° F.
3. Remove wings from marinade and shake off excess marinade. Season all sides of the wings with Traeger Chicken Rub and let sit for 15 minutes before putting wings on the Traeger.
4. In a small bowl, combine the BBQ and chili sauces. Set aside.
5. Cook wings to an internal temperature of 160°F. Remove the wings and toss in chili barbecue sauce. Grill: 225 °F Probe: 160 °F
6. Increase the grill temperature to 375°F and preheat. Once at temperature, place the wings on the Traeger and sear both sides until the internal temperature reaches 165°F. Grill: 375 °F Probe: 165 °F
7. Remove the wings from grill and let rest for 5 minutes. Serve with your favorite side wing dressing or sauce. Enjoy!

Cider-brined Turkey

Servings: 8
Cooking Time: 180 Minutes

Ingredients:
- 1 whole turkey, about 12 to 14lb (4.5 to 5.4kg), thawed if frozen
- 1 white onion, peeled and sliced into quarters
- 1 apple, cut into wedges
- 2 celery stalks, sliced into 2-inch (5cm) pieces
- sprigs of fresh sage, rosemary, parsley, or thyme
- 8 tbsp unsalted butter, at room temperature
- coarse salt
- freshly ground black pepper
- for the brine
- 1 quart (1 liter) apple cider or apple juice
- 3 quarts (3 liters) cold distilled water
- ¾ cup coarse salt
- ½ cup light brown sugar or low-carb substitute
- 3 garlic cloves, peeled and smashed with a chef's knife
- 3 bay leaves

Directions:
1. In a large food-safe bucket, make the brine by combining the apple cider, water, salt, and brown sugar. Stir until the salt and sugar dissolve. Add the garlic and bay leaves. Submerge the turkey in the brine. If it floats, place a resealable bag of ice on top. Refrigerate for at least 8 hours and up to 16 hours.
2. Supply your smoker with wood pellets and follow the start-up procedure. Preheat the grill, with the lid closed, to 350° F.
3. Remove the turkey from the brine and pat dry with paper towels. Discard the brine. Place the onion, apple, celery, and herbs in the main cavity.

Tie the legs together with butcher's twine. Fold the wings behind the back. Rub the outside with butter. Lightly season with salt and pepper.

4. Place the turkey breast side up on a wire rack in a shallow roasting pan. Place the pan on the grate and roast the turkey until the internal temperature in the thickest part of a thigh reaches 165°F (74°C), about 2½ to 3 hours.

5. Transfer the turkey to a cutting board and let rest for 20 minutes. (Save the drippings to make from-scratch turkey gravy.) Carve the turkey and arrange the meat on a large platter before serving.

Bbq Chicken Breasts

Servings: 6
Cooking Time: 25 Minutes

Ingredients:

- 6 boneless, skinless chicken breast
- 1 1/2 Cup Sweet & Heat BBQ Sauce
- salt and pepper
- 1 Tablespoon chopped parsley, for garnish

Directions:

1. Place chicken breasts and 1 cup of Traeger Sweet & Heat BBQ Sauce in a resealable bag or large bowl, and gently turn to cover chicken evenly in the sauce. Marinate in the refrigerator overnight.
2. Supply your smoker with wood pellets and follow the start-up procedure. Preheat the grill, with the lid closed, to 450° F.
3. Remove chicken from marinade and season with salt and pepper.
4. Place chicken directly on the grill grate and cook for 10 minutes on each side flipping once or until internal temperature reaches 150°F.
5. Brush on remaining 1/2 cup of Traeger Sweet & Heat BBQ Sauce while chicken is still on the grill, and continue to cook 5 to 10 minutes longer or until a finished internal temperature of 165°F.
6. Remove chicken from grill and let rest 5 minutes before serving. Sprinkle with chopped parsley. Enjoy!

Spicy Bbq Whole Chicken

Servings: 4
Cooking Time: 180 Minutes

Ingredients:

- 6 Thai chiles
- 2 Tablespoon sweet paprika
- 1 Scotch bonnet pepper
- 2 Tablespoon sugar
- 3 Tablespoon salt
- 1 white onion
- 5 Clove garlic
- 4 Cup grapeseed oil
- 1 whole chicken

Directions:

1. In a food processor or blender, puree the Thai chiles, paprika, Scotch bonnet pepper, sugar, salt, onion, garlic and grapeseed oil together until smooth.
2. Smother the chicken with mixture and let rest in fridge overnight.
3. Supply your smoker with wood pellets and follow the start-up procedure. Preheat the grill, with the lid closed, to 300° F.
4. Place chicken on grill, breast side up and smoke for 3 hours, or until it reaches an internal temperature of 165°F in the breast. Grill: 300 °F Probe: 165 °F
5. Remove from grill and allow to rest for 10 to 15 minutes before slicing. Serve with sides of choice. Enjoy!

Grilled Honey Chicken Kabobs

Servings: 4
Cooking Time: 14 Minutes

Ingredients:
- 1 pound boneless skinless chicken breasts (cut into 1 inch pieces)
- 1/4 cup olive oil
- 1/3 cup soy sauce
- 1/4 cup honey
- 1 teaspoon minced garlic
- salt and pepper to taste
- 1 red bell pepper (cut into 1 inch pieces)
- 1 yellow bell pepper (cut into 1 inch pieces)
- 2 small zucchini (cut into 1 inch slices)
- 1 red onion (cut into 1 inch pieces)
- 1 tablespoon chopped parsley

Directions:
1. In a large bowl combine the olive oil, soy sauce, honey, garlic and salt and pepper, and whisk.
2. Add the chicken, bell peppers, zucchini and red onion to the bowl, tossing to thoroughly coat.
3. Cover and refrigerate for 1 to 8 hours.
4. Soak wooden skewers in cold water for at least 30 minutes. Supply your smoker with wood pellets and follow the start-up procedure. Preheat the grill, with the lid closed, to high heat.
5. Thread the chicken and vegetables onto the skewers.
6. Cook for 5-7 minutes on each side or until chicken is cooked through.
7. To serve, sprinkle with parsley. Enjoy!

Big Game Roast Chicken

Servings: 4
Cooking Time: 60 Minutes

Ingredients:
- 1 whole chicken
- Big Game Rub

Directions:
1. Supply your smoker with wood pellets and follow the start-up procedure. Preheat the grill, with the lid closed, to 375° F.
2. Remove the neck and gizzards from the cavity of the bird. Rinse and wipe the outside and inside of the chicken with a paper towel. Tie chicken legs together with butcher twine and tuck wings.
3. Apply an even coat of the Traeger Big Game Rub to the inside and outside of the chicken.
4. Place chicken on the grill grate and cook for 60 minutes. After an hour, check the temperature of the bird in the thickest part of the leg. The temperature needs to be between 165 and 180°F. Check every 15 minutes if not up to temperature. When the leg reaches desired internal temperature, check the temperature of the breast. The breast needs to reach an internal temperature of 165°F before it is done. Grill: 375 °F Probe: 165 °F
5. Let bird rest for 15 to 20 minutes for slicing. Enjoy!

Baked Prosciutto-wrapped Chicken Breast With Spinach And Boursin

Servings: 4
Cooking Time: 60 Minutes

Ingredients:
- 1 Tablespoon olive oil
- 10 Ounce baby spinach leaves, washed and dried
- 2 Whole packs (5.2 oz) Boursin Garlic & Fine Herbs Gournay Cheese

- 2 Pound boneless, skinless chicken breasts
- Pork & Poultry Rub
- 14 Slices prosciutto

Directions:

1. Heat olive oil in a medium sauté pan. Add spinach and sauté until wilted, about 3 to 5 minutes. Transfer to a strainer and squeeze out excess liquid. Place spinach and cheese in a medium bowl. Mix well and set aside.
2. Butterfly each chicken breast and open like a book. Cover with plastic wrap and using a meat mallet, pound out thinly. Season the chicken with Pork & Poultry Rub.
3. Lay a sheet of plastic wrap about 2 feet long down on a flat, clean surface. Lay down slices of prosciutto, slightly overlapping and double-wide. Place the chicken on top of the prosciutto leaving a 1-1/2 inch border.
4. Spread the spinach mixture on top of the chicken. Roll it up tightly to create a log. Tie off the ends tightly and transfer to the refrigerator. Refrigerate 2 to 3 hours or overnight.
5. Supply your smoker with wood pellets and follow the start-up procedure. Preheat the grill, with the lid closed, to 300° F.
6. Carefully remove the plastic wrap and place directly on the grill grate. Bake for an hour and a half, or until the internal temperature reaches 162°F to 165°F. Remove from Traeger and let rest for 10 minutes before slicing. Enjoy! Grill: 300 °F Probe: 162 °F

Grilled Honey Garlic Wings

Servings: 4
Cooking Time: 60 Minutes

Ingredients:

- 2 1/2 Pound chicken wings
- Pork & Poultry Rub
- 4 Tablespoon butter
- 3 Clove garlic, minced
- 1/4 Cup honey
- 1/2 Cup hot sauce
- 1 1/2 Cup blue cheese or ranch dressing

Directions:

1. Start by segmenting the wings into three pieces, cutting through the joints. Discard the wing tips or save them to make a stock.
2. Lay out the remaining pieces on a rimmed baking sheet lined with nonstick foil or parchment paper. Season well with Traeger Pork & Poultry Rub.
3. Supply your smoker with wood pellets and follow the start-up procedure. Preheat the grill, with the lid closed, to 350° F.
4. Place the baking sheet with wings directly on the grill grate and cook for 45 to 50 minutes or until they are no longer pink at the bone. Grill: 350 °F
5. To make the sauce: Melt butter in a small saucepan. Add the garlic and sauté for 2 to 3 minutes. Add in the honey and hot sauce and cook for a few minutes until completely combined. Keep sauce warm while the wings are cooking.
6. After 45 minutes, pour the spicy honey-garlic sauce over the wings, turning with tongs to coat.
7. Place wings back on the grill and cook for an additional 10 to 15 minutes to set the sauce. Grill: 350 °F
8. Serve with ranch or blue cheese dressing. Enjoy!

APPETIZERS AND SNACKS

Chicken Wings With Teriyaki Glaze

Servings: 4
Cooking Time: 50 Minutes

Ingredients:
- 16 large chicken wings, about 3lb (1.4kg) total
- 1 to 1½ tbsp toasted sesame oil
- for the glaze
- ½ cup light soy sauce or tamari
- ¼ cup sake or sugar-free dark-colored soda
- ¼ cup light brown sugar or low-carb substitute
- 2 tbsp mirin or 1 tbsp honey
- 1 garlic clove, peeled, minced or grated
- 2 tsp minced fresh ginger
- 1 tsp cornstarch mixed with 1 tbsp distilled water (optional)
- for serving
- 1 tbsp toasted sesame seeds
- 2 scallions, trimmed, white and green parts sliced sharply diagonally

Directions:
1. Supply your smoker with wood pellets and follow the start-up procedure. Preheat the grill, with the lid closed, to 350° F.
2. Place the chicken wings in a large bowl, add the sesame oil, and turn the wings to coat thoroughly.
3. Place the wings on the grate at an angle to the bars. Grill for 20 minutes and then turn. Continue to cook until the wings are nicely browned and the meat is no longer pink at the bone, about 20 minutes more.
4. To make the glaze, in a saucepan on the stovetop over medium-high heat, combine the ingredients and bring the mixture to a boil. Reduce the glaze by 1/3, about 6 to 8 minutes. If you prefer your glaze to be glossy and thick, add the cornstarch and water mixture to the glaze and cook until it coats the back of a spoon, about 1 to 2 minutes more.
5. Transfer the wings to an aluminum foil roasting pan. Pour the glaze over them, turning to coat thoroughly. Place the pan on the grate and cook the wings until the glaze sets, about 5 to 10 minutes.
6. Transfer the wings to a platter. Scatter the sesame seeds and scallions over the top. Serve with plenty of napkins.

Bacon-wrapped Jalapeño Poppers

Servings: 12
Cooking Time: 30 Minutes

Ingredients:
- 8 ounces cream cheese, softened
- ½ cup shredded Cheddar cheese
- ¼ cup chopped scallions
- 1 teaspoon chipotle chile powder or regular chili powder
- 1 teaspoon garlic powder
- 1 teaspoon salt
- 18 large jalapeño peppers, stemmed, seeded, and halved lengthwise
- 1 pound bacon (precooked works well)

Directions:
1. Supply your smoker with wood pellets and follow the start-up procedure. Preheat, with the

lid closed, to 350°F. Line a baking sheet with aluminum foil.
2. In a small bowl, combine the cream cheese, Cheddar cheese, scallions, chipotle powder, garlic powder, and salt.
3. Stuff the jalapeño halves with the cheese mixture.
4. Cut the bacon into pieces big enough to wrap around the stuffed pepper halves.
5. Wrap the bacon around the peppers and place on the prepared baking sheet.
6. Put the baking sheet on the grill grate, close the lid, and smoke the peppers for 30 minutes, or until the cheese is melted and the bacon is cooked through and crisp.
7. Let the jalapeño poppers cool for 3 to 5 minutes. Serve warm.

Bacon Pork Pinwheels (kansas Lollipops)

Servings: 4-6
Cooking Time: 20 Minutes

Ingredients:
- 1 Whole Pork Loin, boneless
- To Taste salt and pepper
- To Taste Greek Seasoning
- 4 Slices bacon
- To Taste The Ultimate BBQ Sauce

Directions:
1. When ready to cook, start the smoker and set temperature to 500F. Preheat, lid closed, for 10 to 15 minutes.
2. Trim pork loin of any unwanted silver skin or fat. Using a sharp knife, cut pork loin length wise, into 4 long strips.
3. Lay pork flat, then season with salt, pepper and Cavender's Greek Seasoning.
4. Flip the pork strips over and layer bacon on unseasoned side. Begin tightly rolling the pork strips, with bacon being rolled up on the inside.
5. Secure a skewer all the way through each pork roll to secure it in place. Set the pork rolls down on grill and cook for 15 minutes.
6. Brush BBQ Sauce over the pork. Turn each skewer over, then coat the other side. Let pork cook for another 5-10 minutes, depending on thickness of your pork. Enjoy!

Bayou Wings With Cajun Rémoulade

Servings: 8
Cooking Time: 40 Minutes

Ingredients:
- 16 large whole chicken wings or 32 drumettes and flats, about 3lb (1.4kg) total
- for the rub
- 1 tbsp kosher salt
- 1 tsp freshly ground black pepper
- 1 tsp paprika
- ½ tsp ground cayenne, plus more
- ½ tsp garlic powder
- ½ tsp celery salt
- ½ tsp dried thyme
- 2 tbsp vegetable oil
- for the rémoulade
- 1¼ cups reduced-fat mayo
- ¼ cup Creole-style or whole grain mustard
- 2 tbsp horseradish
- 2 tbsp pickle relish
- 1 tbsp freshly squeezed lemon juice
- 1 tsp paprika, plus more
- 1 tsp hot sauce, plus more
- 1 tsp Worcestershire sauce
- coarse salt

- for serving
- lemon wedges
- pickled okra (optional)

Directions:

1. Supply your smoker with wood pellets and follow the start-up procedure. Preheat the grill, with the lid closed, to 350° F.

2. If using whole wings, cut through the two joints, separating them into drumettes, flats, and wing tips. (Discard the wing tips or save them for chicken stock.) Alternatively, leave the wings whole. Place the chicken in a resealable plastic bag.

3. In a small bowl, make the rub by combining the ingredients. Mix well. Pour the rub over the wings and toss them to thoroughly coat. Refrigerate for 2 hours.

4. In a small bowl, make the Cajun rémoulade by whisking together the mayo, mustard, horseradish, pickle relish, lemon juice, paprika, hot sauce, and Worcestershire. Season with salt to taste. The mixture should be highly seasoned. Transfer to a serving bowl and lightly dust with paprika. Cover and refrigerate until ready to serve.

5. Remove the wings from the refrigerator and allow the excess marinade to drip off. Place the wings on the grate at an angle to the bars. Grill for 20 minutes and then turn. (They'll brown more evenly but will also have less of a tendency to stick.) Continue to cook until the wings are nicely browned and the meat is no longer pink at the bone, about 20 minutes more.

6. Remove the wings from the grill and pile them on a platter. Serve with the Cajun rémoulade, lemon wedges, and pickled okra (if using).

Pulled Pork Loaded Nachos

Servings: 4
Cooking Time: 10 Minutes

Ingredients:
- 2 cups leftover smoked pulled pork
- 1 small sweet onion, diced
- 1 medium tomato, diced
- 1 jalapeño pepper, seeded and diced
- 1 garlic clove, minced
- 1 teaspoon salt
- 1 teaspoon freshly ground black pepper
- 1 bag tortilla chips
- 1 cup shredded Cheddar cheese
- ½ cup The Ultimate BBQ Sauce, divided
- ½ cup shredded jalapeño Monterey Jack cheese
- Juice of ½ lime
- 1 avocado, halved, pitted, and sliced
- 2 tablespoons sour cream
- 1 tablespoon chopped fresh cilantro

Directions:

1. Supply your smoker with wood pellets and follow the start-up procedure. Preheat, with the lid closed, to 375°F.

2. Heat the pulled pork in the microwave.

3. In a medium bowl, combine the onion, tomato, jalapeño, garlic, salt, and pepper, and set aside.

4. Arrange half of the tortilla chips in a large cast iron skillet. Spread half of the warmed pork on top and cover with the Cheddar cheese. Top with half of the onion-jalapeño mixture, then drizzle with ¼ cup of barbecue sauce.

5. Layer on the remaining tortilla chips, then the remaining pork and the Monterey Jack cheese. Top with the remaining onion-jalapeño mixture

and drizzle with the remaining ¼ cup of barbecue sauce.

6. Place the skillet on the grill, close the lid, and smoke for about 10 minutes, or until the cheese is melted and bubbly. (Watch to make sure your chips don't burn!)

7. Squeeze the lime juice over the nachos, top with the avocado slices and sour cream, and garnish with the cilantro before serving hot.

Citrus-infused Marinated Olives

Servings: 6
Cooking Time: 30 Minutes

Ingredients:
- 1½ cups mixed brined olives, with pits
- ½ cup extra virgin olive oil
- 1 tbsp freshly squeezed lemon juice
- 1 garlic clove, peeled and thinly sliced
- 1 tsp smoked Spanish paprika
- 2 sprigs of fresh rosemary
- 2 sprigs of fresh thyme
- 2 bay leaves, fresh or dried
- 1 small dried red chili pepper, deseeded and flesh crumbled, or ¼ tsp crushed red pepper flakes
- 3 strips of orange zest
- 3 strips of lemon zest

Directions:
1. Supply your smoker with wood pellets and follow the start-up procedure. Preheat the grill, with the lid closed, to 180° F.
2. Drain the olives, reserving 1 tablespoon of brine. Spread the olives in a single layer in an aluminum foil roasting pan. Place the pan on the grate and cook the olives for 30 minutes, stirring the olives or shaking the pan once or twice.
3. In a small saucepan on the stovetop over low heat, warm the olive oil. Whisk in the lemon juice and the reserved 1 tablespoon of brine. Stir in the garlic and paprika. Add the rosemary, thyme, bay leaves, chili pepper, and orange and lemon zests. Warm over low heat for 10 minutes. Remove the saucepan from the heat.
4. Transfer the olives and olive oil mixture to a pint jar. Tuck the aromatics around the sides of the jar. Let cool and then cover and refrigerate for up to 5 days. Let the olives come to room temperature before serving.

Chorizo Queso Fundido

Servings: 4-6
Cooking Time: 20 Minutes

Ingredients:
- 1 poblano chile
- 1 cup chopped queso quesadilla or queso Oaxaca
- 1 cup shredded Monterey Jack cheese
- ¼ cup milk
- 1 tablespoon all-purpose flour
- 2 (4-ounce) links Mexican chorizo sausage, casings removed
- ⅓ cup beer
- 1 tablespoon unsalted butter
- 1 small red onion, chopped
- ½ cup whole kernel corn
- 2 serrano chiles or jalapeño peppers, stemmed, seeded, and coarsely chopped
- 1 tablespoon minced garlic
- 1 tablespoon freshly squeezed lime juice
- 1 teaspoon ground cumin
- 1 teaspoon salt
- 1 teaspoon freshly ground black pepper
- 1 tablespoon chopped fresh cilantro
- 1 tablespoon chopped scallions
- Tortilla chips, for serving

Directions:
1. Supply your smoker with wood pellets and follow the start-up procedure. Preheat, with the lid closed, to 350°F.
2. On the smoker or over medium-high heat on the stove top, place the poblano directly on the grate (or burner) to char for 1 to 2 minutes, turning as needed. Remove from heat and place in a closed-up lunch-size paper bag for 2 minutes to sweat and further loosen the skin.
3. Remove the skin and coarsely chop the poblano, removing the seeds; set aside.
4. In a bowl, combine the queso quesadilla, Monterey Jack, milk, and flour; set aside.
5. On the stove top, in a cast iron skillet over medium heat, cook and crumble the chorizo for about 2 minutes.
6. Transfer the cooked chorizo to a small, grill-safe pan and place over indirect heat on the smoker.
7. Place the cast iron skillet on the preheated grill grate. Pour in the beer and simmer for a few minutes, loosening and stirring in any remaining sausage bits from the pan.
8. Add the butter to the pan, then add the cheese mixture a little at a time, stirring constantly.
9. When the cheese is smooth, stir in the onion, corn, serrano chiles, garlic, lime juice, cuvmin, salt, and pepper. Stir in the reserved chopped charred poblano.
10. Close the lid and smoke for 15 to 20 minutes to infuse the queso with smoke flavor and further cook the vegetables.
11. When the cheese is bubbly, top with the chorizo mixture and garnish with the cilantro and scallions.
12. Serve the chorizo queso fundido hot with tortilla chips.

Grilled Guacamole

Servings: 6
Cooking Time: 30 Minutes

Ingredients:
- 3 large avocados, halved and pitted
- 1 lime, halved
- ½ jalapeño, deseeded and deveined
- ½ small white or red onion, peeled
- 2 garlic cloves, peeled and skewered on a toothpick
- 1 tsp coarse salt, plus more
- 1½ tbsp reduced-fat mayo
- 2 tbsp chopped fresh cilantro
- 2 tbsp crumbled queso fresco (optional)
- tortilla chips

Directions:
1. Supply your smoker with wood pellets and follow the start-up procedure. Preheat the grill, with the lid closed, to 225° F.
2. Place the avocados, lime, jalapeño, and onion cut sides down on the grate. Use the toothpicks to balance the garlic cloves between the bars. Smoke for 30 minutes. (You want the vegetables to retain most of their rawness.)
3. Transfer everything to a cutting board. Remove the garlic cloves from the toothpick and roughly chop. Sprinkle with the salt and continue to mince the garlic until it begins to form a paste. Scrape the garlic and salt into a large bowl.
4. Scoop the avocado flesh from the peels into the bowl. Squeeze the juice of ½ lime over the avocado. Mash the avocados but leave them somewhat chunky. Finely dice the jalapeño. Dice 2 tablespoons of onion. (Reserve the remaining

onion for another use.) Add the jalapeño, onion, mayo, and cilantro to the bowl. Stir gently to combine. Taste for seasoning, adding more salt, lime juice, and jalapeño as desired.

5. Transfer the guacamole to a serving bowl. Top with the queso fresco (if using). Serve with tortilla chips.

Pigs In A Blanket

Servings: 4-6
Cooking Time: 15 Minutes

Ingredients:
- 2 Tablespoon Poppy Seeds
- 1 Tablespoon Dried Minced Onion
- 2 Teaspoon garlic, minced
- 2 Tablespoon Sesame Seeds
- 1 Teaspoon salt
- 8 Ounce Original Crescent Dough
- 1/4 Cup Dijon mustard
- 1 Large egg, beaten

Directions:
1. When ready to cook, start your smoker at 350 degrees F, and preheat with lid closed, 10 to 15 minutes.
2. Mix together poppy seeds, dried minced onion, dried minced garlic, salt and sesame seeds. Set aside.
3. Cut each triangle of crescent roll dough into thirds lengthwise, making 3 small strips from each roll.
4. Brush the dough strips lightly with Dijon mustard. Put the mini hot dogs on 1 end of the dough and roll up.
5. Arrange them, seam side down, on a greased baking pan. Brush with egg wash and sprinkle with seasoning mixture.
6. Bake in smoker until golden brown, about 12 to 15 minutes.
7. Serve with mustard or dipping sauce of your choice. Enjoy!

Simple Cream Cheese Sausage Balls

Servings: 5
Cooking Time: 30 Minutes

Ingredients:
- 1 pound ground hot sausage, uncooked
- 8 ounces cream cheese, softened
- 1 package mini filo dough shells

Directions:
1. Supply your smoker with wood pellets and follow the start-up procedure. Preheat, with the lid closed, to 350°F.
2. In a large bowl, using your hands, thoroughly mix together the sausage and cream cheese until well blended.
3. Place the filo dough shells on a rimmed perforated pizza pan or into a mini muffin tin.
4. Roll the sausage and cheese mixture into 1-inch balls and place into the filo shells.
5. Place the pizza pan or mini muffin tin on the grill, close the lid, and smoke the sausage balls for 30 minutes, or until cooked through and the sausage is no longer pink.
6. Plate and serve warm.

Deviled Eggs With Smoked Paprika

Servings: 6
Cooking Time: 30 Minutes

Ingredients:
- 6 large eggs

- 3 tbsp reduced-fat mayo, plus more
- 1 tsp Dijon or yellow mustard
- ½ tsp Spanish smoked paprika or regular paprika, plus more
- dash of hot sauce
- coarse salt
- freshly ground black pepper
- for garnishing
- small sprigs of fresh parsley, dill, tarragon, or cilantro
- chopped chives
- minced scallions
- Mustard Caviar
- sliced green or black olives
- celery leaves
- sliced radishes
- diced bell peppers
- sliced cherry tomatoes
- fresh or pickled jalapeños
- sliced or diced pickles
- slivers of sun-dried tomatoes
- bacon crumbles
- smoked salmon
- Hawaiian black salt
- Caviar

Directions:

1. Supply your smoker with wood pellets and follow the start-up procedure. Preheat the grill, with the lid closed, to 180° F.

2. On the stovetop over medium-high heat, bring a saucepan of water to a boil. (Make sure there's enough water in the saucepan to cover the eggs by 1 inch [5cm].) Use a slotted spoon to gently lower the eggs into the water. Lower the heat to maintain a simmer. Set a timer for 13 minutes.

3. Prepare an ice bath by combining ice and cold water in a large bowl. Carefully transfer the eggs to the ice bath when the timer goes off.

4. When the eggs are cool enough to handle, gently tap them all over to crack the shell. Carefully peel the eggs. Rinse under cold running water to remove any clinging bits of shell, but don't dry the eggs. (A damp surface will help the smoke adhere to the egg whites.)

5. Place the eggs on the grate and smoke until the eggs take on a light brown patina from the smoke, about 25 minutes. Transfer the eggs to a cutting board, handling them as little as possible.

6. Slice each egg in half lengthwise with a sharp knife. Wipe any yolk off the blade before slicing the next egg. Gently remove the yolks and place them in a food processor. Pulse to break up the yolks. Add the mayo, mustard, paprika, and hot sauce. Season with salt and pepper to taste. Pulse until the filling is smooth. Add additional mayo 1 teaspoon at a time if the mixture is a little dry. (It shouldn't be too loose either.)

7. Spoon the filling into each egg half or pipe it in using a small resealable plastic bag. You can also use a pastry bag fitted with a fluted tip.

8. Place the eggs on a platter and lightly dust with paprika. Accompany with one or more of the suggested garnishes.

Smoked Cashews

Servings: 6
Cooking Time: 60 Minutes

Ingredients:

- 1 pound roasted, salted cashews

Directions:

1. Supply your smoker with wood pellets and follow the start-up procedure. Preheat the grill, with the lid closed, to 120°F.
2. Pour the cashews onto a rimmed baking sheet and smoke for 1 hour, stirring once about halfway through the smoking time.
3. Remove the cashews from the grill, let cool, and store in an airtight container for as long as you can resist.

Pig Pops (sweet-hot Bacon On A Stick)

Servings: 24
Cooking Time: 30 Minutes

Ingredients:
- Nonstick cooking spray, oil, or butter, for greasing
- 2 pounds thick-cut bacon (24 slices)
- 24 metal skewers
- 1 cup packed light brown sugar
- 2 to 3 teaspoons cayenne pepper
- ½ cup maple syrup, divided

Directions:
1. Supply your smoker with wood pellets and follow the start-up procedure. Preheat, with the lid closed, to 350°F.
2. Coat a disposable aluminum foil baking sheet with cooking spray, oil, or butter.
3. Thread each bacon slice onto a metal skewer and place on the prepared baking sheet.
4. In a medium bowl, stir together the brown sugar and cayenne.
5. Baste the top sides of the bacon with ¼ cup of maple syrup.
6. Sprinkle half of the brown sugar mixture over the bacon.
7. Place the baking sheet on the grill, close the lid, and smoke for 15 to 30 minutes.
8. Using tongs, flip the bacon skewers. Baste with the remaining ¼ cup of maple syrup and top with the remaining brown sugar mixture.
9. Continue smoking with the lid closed for 10 to 15 minutes, or until crispy. You can eyeball the bacon and smoke to your desired doneness, but the actual ideal internal temperature for bacon is 155°F
10. Using tongs, carefully remove the bacon skewers from the grill. Let cool completely before handling.

Chuckwagon Beef Jerky

Servings: 6
Cooking Time: 300 Minutes

Ingredients:
- 2½lb (1.2kg) boneless top or bottom round steak, sirloin tip, flank steak, or venison
- 1 cup sugar-free dark-colored soda
- 1 cup cold brewed coffee
- ½ cup light soy sauce
- ¼ cup Worcestershire sauce
- 2 tbsp whiskey (optional)
- 2 tsp chili powder
- 1½ tsp garlic salt
- 1 tsp onion powder
- 1 tsp pink curing salt

Directions:
1. Slice the meat into ¼-inch-thick (.5cm) strips, trimming off any visible fat or gristle. (Slice against the grain for more tender jerky and with the grain for chewier jerky.) Place the meat in a large resealable plastic bag.
2. In a small bowl, whisk together the soda, coffee, soy sauce, Worcestershire sauce, whiskey

(if using), chili powder, garlic salt, onion powder, and curing salt (if using). Whisk until the salt dissolves. Pour the mixture over the meat and reseal the bag. Refrigerate for 24 to 48 hours, turning the bag several times to redistribute the brine.

3. Supply your smoker with wood pellets and follow the start-up procedure. Preheat the grill, with the lid closed, to 150° F.

4. Drain the meat and discard the brine. Place the strips of meat in a single layer on paper towels and blot any excess moisture.

5. Place the meat in a single layer on the grate and smoke for 4 to 5 hours, turning once or twice. (If you're aware of hot spots on your grate, rotate the strips so they smoke evenly.) To test for doneness, bend one or two pieces in the middle. They should be dry but still somewhat pliant. Or simply eat a piece to see if it's done to your liking.

6. For the best texture, when you remove the meat from the grill, place the still-warm jerky in a resealable plastic bag and let rest for 30 minutes. (You might see condensation form on the inside of the bag, but the moisture will be reabsorbed by the meat.) Or let the meat cool completely and then store in a resealable plastic bag or covered container. The jerky will last a few days at room temperature but will last longer (up to 2 weeks) if refrigerated.

Smoked Cheese

Servings: 4
Cooking Time: 150 Minutes

Ingredients:
- 1 (2-pound) block medium Cheddar cheese, or your favorite cheese, quartered lengthwise

Directions:

1. Supply your smoker with wood pellets and follow the start-up procedure. Preheat the grill, with the lid closed, to 90°F.

2. Place the cheese directly on the grill grate and smoke for 2 hours, 30 minutes, checking frequently to be sure it's not melting. If the cheese begins to melt, try flipping it. If that doesn't help, remove it from the grill and refrigerate for about 1 hour and then return it to the cold smoker.

3. Remove the cheese, place it in a zip-top bag, and refrigerate overnight.

4. Slice the cheese and serve with crackers, or grate it and use for making a smoked mac and cheese.

Roasted Red Pepper Dip

Servings: 8
Cooking Time: 45 Minutes

Ingredients:
- 4 red bell peppers, halved, destemmed, and deseeded
- 1 cup English walnuts, divided
- 1 small white onion, peeled and coarsely chopped
- 2 garlic cloves, peeled and smashed with a chef's knife
- ¼ cup extra virgin olive oil, plus more
- 1 tbsp balsamic vinegar or balsamic glaze
- 1 tsp honey (eliminate if using balsamic glaze)
- 1 tsp coarse salt, plus more
- 1 tsp ground cumin
- 1 tsp smoked paprika
- ½ to 1 tsp Aleppo red pepper flakes, plus more
- ¼ cup fresh white breadcrumbs (optional)
- distilled water (optional)
- assorted crudités or wedges of pita bread

Directions:

1. Supply your smoker with wood pellets and follow the start-up procedure. Preheat the grill, with the lid closed, to 400° F.
2. Place the peppers skin side down on the grate and grill until the skins blister and the flesh softens, about 30 minutes. Transfer the peppers to a bowl and cover with plastic wrap. Let cool to room temperature. Remove the skins with a paring knife or your fingers. Coarsely chop or tear the peppers.
3. Place ¾ cup of walnuts in an aluminum foil roasting pan. Place the pan on the grate and toast for 10 to 15 minutes, stirring twice. Remove the pan from the grill and let the walnuts cool.
4. Place the peppers, onion, garlic, and walnuts in a food processor fitted with the chopping blade. Pulse several times. Add the olive oil, balsamic vinegar, honey, salt, cumin, paprika, and red pepper flakes. Process until the mixture is fairly smooth. Taste for seasoning, adding more salt or red pepper flakes (if desired). (If the mixture is too loose, add breadcrumbs until the texture is to your liking. If it's too thick, add olive oil or water 1 tablespoon at a time.)
5. Transfer the dip to a serving bowl. Use the back of a spoon to make a shallow depression in the center. Top with the remaining ¼ cup of walnuts and drizzle olive oil in the depression. Serve with crudités or pita bread.

Delicious Deviled Crab Appetizer

Servings: 30
Cooking Time: 10 Minutes

Ingredients:
- Nonstick cooking spray, oil, or butter, for greasing
- 1 cup panko breadcrumbs, divided
- 1 cup canned corn, drained
- ½ cup chopped scallions, divided
- ½ red bell pepper, finely chopped
- 16 ounces jumbo lump crabmeat
- ¾ cup mayonnaise, divided
- 1 egg, beaten
- 1 teaspoon salt
- 1 teaspoon freshly ground black pepper
- 2 teaspoons cayenne pepper, divided
- Juice of 1 lemon

Directions:

1. Supply your smoker with wood pellets and follow the start-up procedure. Preheat, with the lid closed, to 425°F.
2. Spray three 12-cup mini muffin pans with cooking spray and divide ½ cup of the panko between 30 of the muffin cups, pressing into the bottoms and up the sides. (Work in batches, if necessary, depending on the number of pans you have.)
3. In a medium bowl, combine the corn, ¼ cup of scallions, the bell pepper, crabmeat, half of the mayonnaise, the egg, salt, pepper, and 1 teaspoon of cayenne pepper.
4. Gently fold in the remaining ½ cup of breadcrumbs and divide the mixture between the prepared mini muffin cups.
5. Place the pans on the grill grate, close the lid, and smoke for 10 minutes, or until golden brown.
6. In a small bowl, combine the lemon juice and the remaining mayonnaise, scallions, and cayenne pepper to make a sauce.
7. Brush the tops of the mini crab cakes with the sauce and serve hot.

Smoked Turkey Sandwich

Servings: 1
Cooking Time: 15 Minutes

Ingredients:
- 2 slices sourdough bread
- 2 tablespoons butter, at room temperature
- 2 (1-ounce) slices Swiss cheese
- 4 ounces leftover Smoked Turkey
- 1 teaspoon garlic salt

Directions:
1. Supply your smoker with wood pellets and follow the start-up procedure. Preheat the grill, with the lid closed, to 375°F.
2. Coat one side of each bread slice with 1 tablespoon of butter and sprinkle the buttered sides with garlic salt.
3. Place 1 slice of cheese on each unbuttered side of the bread, and then put the turkey on the cheese.
4. Close the sandwich, buttered sides out, and place it directly on the grill grate. Cook for 5 minutes. Flip the sandwich and cook for 5 minutes more. Remove the sandwich from the grill, cut it in half, and serve.

Sriracha & Maple Cashews

Servings: 10
Cooking Time: 60 Minutes

Ingredients:
- 2 tbsp unsalted butter
- 3 tbsp pure maple syrup
- 1 tbsp sriracha
- 1 tsp coarse salt (use only if nuts are unsalted)
- 2½ cups unsalted cashews

Directions:

1. Supply your smoker with wood pellets and follow the start-up procedure. Preheat the grill, with the lid closed, to 250° F.
2. In a small saucepan on the stovetop over low heat, melt the butter. Add the maple syrup, sriracha, and salt (if using). Stir until combined. Add the nuts and stir gently to coat thoroughly.
3. Spread the nuts in a single layer in an aluminum foil roasting pan coated with cooking spray. Place the pan on the grate and smoke the nuts until they're lightly toasted, about 1 hour, stirring once or twice.
4. Remove the pan from the grill and let the nuts cool for 15 minutes. They'll be sticky at first but will crisp up. Break them up with your fingers and store at room temperature in an airtight container, such as a lidded glass jar.

Jalapeño Poppers With Chipotle Sour Cream

Servings: 8
Cooking Time: 45 Minutes

Ingredients:
- 3 strips of thin-sliced bacon
- 12 large jalapeños, red, green, or a mix
- 8oz (225g) light cream cheese, at room temperature
- 1 cup shredded pepper Jack, Monterey Jack, or Cheddar cheese
- 1 tsp chili powder
- ½ tsp garlic salt
- smoked paprika
- for the sour cream
- 1¼ cups light sour cream
- juice of ½ lime

- ½ to 1 canned chipotle peppers in adobo sauce, finely minced, plus 1 tsp of sauce, plus more
- 1 tbsp minced fresh cilantro leaves
- ½ tsp coarse salt, plus more

Directions:
1. Supply your smoker with wood pellets and follow the start-up procedure. Preheat the grill, with the lid closed, to 375° F.
2. Line a rimmed sheet pan with aluminum foil and place a wire rack on top. Place the bacon in a single layer on the wire rack. Place the pan on the grate and grill until the bacon is crisp and golden brown, about 20 minutes. Transfer the bacon to paper towels to cool and then crumble. Set aside.
3. In a small bowl, make the chipotle sour cream by whisking together the ingredients. Add more salt, chipotle peppers, or adobe sauce to taste. Cover and refrigerate.
4. Slice the jalapeños lengthwise through their stems. Scrape out the veins and seeds with the edge of a small metal spoon.
5. In a small bowl, beat together the cream cheese, shredded cheese, chili powder, and garlic salt. Stir in the crumbled bacon. Mound the cream cheese mixture in the jalapeño halves. Line another rimmed sheet pan with aluminum foil and place a wire rack on top. Place the jalapeños filled side up in a single layer on the wire rack.
6. Place the sheet pan on the grate and roast the jalapeños until the filling has melted and the peppers have softened, about 20 to 25 minutes. (They should no longer look bright in color.) Remove the pan from the grill and let the peppers rest for 5 minutes.
7. Transfer the poppers to a platter and lightly dust with paprika. Serve with the chipotle sour cream.

Cold-smoked Cheese

Servings: 6
Cooking Time: 180 Minutes

Ingredients:
- 2lb (1kg) well-chilled hard or semi-hard cheese, such as:
- Edam
- Gouda
- Cheddar
- Monterey Jack
- pepper Jack
- goat cheese
- fresh mozzarella
- Muenster
- aged Parmigiano-Reggiano
- Gruyère
- blue cheese

Directions:
1. Unwrap the cheese and remove any protective wax or coating. Cut into 4-ounce (110g) portions to increase the surface area.
2. If possible, move your smoker to a shady area. Place 1 resealable plastic bag filled with ice on top of the drip pan. This is especially important on a warm day because you want to keep the interior temperature of the grill between 70 and 90°F (21 and 32°C) or below.
3. Place a grill mat on one side of the grate. Place the cheese on the mat and allow space between each piece.
4. Fill your smoking tube or pellet maze (see Cast Iron Skillets and Grill Pans) with pellets or sawdust and light according to the manufacturer's

instructions. Place the smoking tube on the grate near—but not on—the grill mat. When the tube is smoking consistently, close the grill lid.

5. Smoke the cheese for 1 to 3 hours, replacing the pellets or sawdust and ice if necessary. Monitor the temperature and make sure the cheese isn't beginning to melt. Carefully lift the mat with the cheese to a rimmed baking sheet and let the cheese cool completely before handling.

6. Package the smoked cheese in cheese storage paper or bags or vacuum-seal the cheese, labeling each. (While you can wrap the cheese tightly in plastic wrap, the cheese will spoil faster.) Let the cheese rest for at least 2 to 3 days before eating. It will be even better after 2 weeks.

COCKTAILS RECIPES

Smoked Eggnog

Servings: 4
Cooking Time: 60 Minutes

Ingredients:
- 2 Cup whole milk
- 1 Cup heavy cream
- 4 egg yolk
- Cup sugar
- 3 Ounce bourbon
- 1 Teaspoon vanilla extract
- 1 Teaspoon nutmeg
- 4 egg white
- whipped cream

Directions:
1. Plan ahead, this recipe requires chill time.
2. Supply your smoker with wood pellets and follow the start-up procedure. Preheat the grill, with the lid closed, to 180° F.
3. Pour the milk and the cream into a baking pan and smoke on the Traeger for 60 minutes. Grill: 180 °F
4. Meanwhile, in the bowl of a stand mixer, beat the egg yolks until they lighten in color. Gradually add 1/3 cup sugar and continue to beat until sugar completely dissolves.
5. After the milk and cream have smoked, add them along with the bourbon, vanilla and nutmeg into the egg mixture and stir to combine.
6. Place the egg whites in the bowl of a stand mixer and beat to soft peaks. When you lift the beaters the whites will make a peak that slightly curls down.
7. With the mixer still running, gradually add 1 tablespoon of sugar and beat until stiff peaks form.
8. Gently fold the egg whites into the cream mixture and then whisk to thoroughly combine.
9. Chill eggnog for a couple hours to let the flavors meld. Garnish with a dash of nutmeg and whipped cream on top. Enjoy!

Garden Gimlet Cocktail

Servings: 2
Cooking Time: 45 Minutes

Ingredients:
- 2 Cup honey
- 4 lemons, zested
- 4 Sprig rosemary, plus more for garnish
- 1/2 Cup water
- 4 Slices cucumber
- 1 1/2 Ounce lime juice
- 3 Ounce vodka

Directions:
1. Supply your smoker with wood pellets and follow the start-up procedure. Preheat the grill, with the lid closed, to 180° F.
2. To make smoked lemon and rosemary honey syrup, thin 1 cup honey by adding 1/4 cup water to a shallow pan. Add lemon zest and 2 sprigs rosemary.
3. Place the pan directly on the grill grate and smoke 45 minutes to an hour. Remove from heat, strain and cool. Grill: 180 °F
4. In a cocktail shaker, muddle the cucumbers and 1oz of the smoked lemon and rosemary honey syrup.
5. After muddling, add lime juice, vodka, and ice. Shake and double strain into a coup glass.
6. Garnish with a sprig of rosemary. Enjoy!

Strawberry Mule Cocktail

Servings: 2
Cooking Time: 15 Minutes

Ingredients:
- 8 grilled strawberries, plus more for serving
- 3 Ounce vodka
- 1 Ounce Smoked Simple Syrup
- 1 Ounce lemon juice
- 6 Ounce ginger beer
- fresh mint leaves

Directions:
1. Supply your smoker with wood pellets and follow the start-up procedure. Preheat the grill, with the lid closed, to 400° F.
2. Place strawberries directly on the grill grate and cook 15 minutes or until grill marks appear. Grill: 400 °F
3. For the cocktail: Add vodka, grilled strawberries, Traeger Smoked Simple Syrup and lemon juice to a shaker. Shake vigorously.
4. Double strain into a fresh glass or copper mug with crushed ice.
5. Top with ginger beer and garnish with extra grilled strawberries and fresh mint. Enjoy!

Bacon Old-fashioned Cocktail

Servings: 2
Cooking Time: 20 Minutes

Ingredients:
- 16 Slices bacon
- 1/2 Cup warm water (110°F to 115°F)
- 1500 mL bourbon
- 1/2 Fluid Ounce maple syrup
- 4 Dash Angostura bitters
- 2 fresh orange peel

Directions:
1. Smoke bacon prior to making Old Fashioned using this recipe for Applewood Smoked Bacon.
2. To Make Bacon: Supply your smoker with wood pellets and follow the start-up procedure. Preheat the grill, with the lid closed, to 325° F.
3. Place bacon in a single layer on a cooling rack that fits inside a baking sheet pan. Cook in Traeger for 15-20 minutes or until bacon is browned and crispy. Reserve bacon for later. Let the fat cool slightly; you'll use the fat to infuse the bourbon. Grill: 325 °F
4. Combine 1/4 cup of warm (not hot) liquid bacon fat with the entire contents of a 750ml bottle of bourbon in a glass or heavy plastic container.
5. Use a fork to stir well. Let it sit on the counter for a few hours, stirring every so often.
6. After about four hours, put bourbon fat mixture into the freezer. After about an hour, the fat will congeal and you can simply scoop it out with a spoon. You can fine-strain the mixture through a sieve to remove all fat if desired.
7. Combine ingredients with ice and stir until cold. Strain over fresh ice in an Old Fashioned glass and garnish with reserved bacon and orange peel. Enjoy!

Smoked Ice Mojito Slurpee

Servings: 2
Cooking Time: 30 Minutes

Ingredients:
- water
- 1 Cup white rum
- 1/2 Cup lime juice
- 1/4 Cup Smoked Simple Syrup
- 12 Whole fresh mint leaves
- 4 Sprig mint

- 4 Whole lime wedge, for garnish

Directions:
1. Supply your smoker with wood pellets and follow the start-up procedure. Preheat the grill, with the lid closed, to 180° F.
2. For optimal flavor, use Super Smoke if available. Grill: 180 °F
3. Remove water from grill and pour smoked water into ice cube trays. Place in freezer until frozen.
4. Add rum, lime juice, Traeger Smoked Simple Syrup, mint and smoked ice to a blender.
5. Blend until a slushy consistency and pour into glasses.
6. Garnish with a mint sprig and lime wedge. Enjoy!

Smoked Hibiscus Sparkler

Servings: 4
Cooking Time: 30 Minutes

Ingredients:
- 1/2 Cup sugar
- 2 Tablespoon dried hibiscus flowers
- 1 Bottle sparkling wine
- crystallized ginger, for garnish

Directions:
1. Supply your smoker with wood pellets and follow the start-up procedure. Preheat the grill, with the lid closed, to 180° F.
2. Place water in a shallow baking dish and place directly on the grill grate. Smoke the water for 30 minutes or until desired smoke flavor is achieved. Grill: 180 °F
3. Pour water into a small saucepan and add sugar and hibiscus flowers. Bring to a simmer over medium heat and cook until sugar is dissolved.
4. Strain out the hibiscus flowers and transfer your simple syrup to a small container and refrigerate until chilled.
5. Pour 1/2 ounce smoked hibiscus simple syrup in the bottom of a champagne glass and top with sparkling wine.
6. Drop in a few pieces of crystallized ginger to garnish. Enjoy!

Traeger Gin & Tonic

Servings: 2
Cooking Time: 45 Minutes

Ingredients:
- 1/2 Cup berries
- 2 orange, sliced
- 4 Tablespoon granulated sugar
- 3 Ounce gin
- 1 Cup tonic water
- 2 Sprig fresh mint, for garnish

Directions:
1. Supply your smoker with wood pellets and follow the start-up procedure. Preheat the grill, with the lid closed, to 180° F.
2. For the Smoked Berries: Spread mixed fresh berries on a sheet pan and place directly on the grill grate. Smoke for 30 minutes then remove from grill. Grill: 180 °F
3. For the Orange Slices: Increase the grill temperature to 450°F and preheat, lid closed for 15 minutes. Grill: 450 °F
4. Toss the orange slices with granulated sugar and place directly on grill grate. Cook for about 5 minutes, turning once or until the slices have developed grill marks. Grill: 450 °F
5. Pour gin into a glass, add ice and berries, then top with tonic water. Garnish with a fresh mint sprig and grilled orange wheel. Enjoy!

Grilled Peach Smash Cocktail

Servings: 2
Cooking Time: 10 Minutes

Ingredients:
- 2 peach, sliced and grilled
- 10 fresh mint leaves
- 1 1/2 Ounce Smoked Simple Syrup
- 4 Ounce bourbon
- 2 mint sprig, for garnish

Directions:
1. Supply your smoker with wood pellets and follow the start-up procedure. Preheat the grill, with the lid closed, to 375° F.
2. Cut the peach into 6 slices and brush with Traeger Smoked Simple Syrup. Place directly on the grill grate and cook 10 to 12 minutes or until peaches soften and get grill marks. Grill: 375 °F
3. In a mixing glass, add 3 slices of grilled peaches, 5 mint leaves and Traeger Smoked Simple Syrup.
4. Muddle ingredients to release oils of the mint and juices from the grilled peaches. Add bourbon and crushed ice.
5. Shake and pour into a stemless wine glass. Top off with more crushed ice. Garnish with a grilled peach and mint sprig. Enjoy!

Smoked Pineapple Hotel Nacional Cocktail

Servings: 2
Cooking Time: 20 Minutes

Ingredients:
- 2 pineapple
- 1/2 Cup water
- 1/2 Cup sugar
- 3 Fluid Ounce white rum
- 1 1/2 Fluid Ounce lime juice
- 1 1/2 Fluid Ounce Pineapple Syrup
- 1 Fluid Ounce apricot brandy
- 2 Dash Angostura bitters

Directions:
1. For the Syrup: Supply your smoker with wood pellets and follow the start-up procedure. Preheat the grill, with the lid closed, to 180° F.
2. Trim both ends of the pineapple, discard the ends. Cut the pineapple into slices about 3/4" thick. Don't worry about the skin, it doesn't hurt to leave it on. Place the pineapple slices on the grill and smoke for about 15 minutes on each sideTrim both ends of the pineapple and discard the ends. Cut the pineapple into slices about 3/4 inch thick. Don't worry about the skin, it doesn't hurt to leave it on. Place the pineapple slices on the grill and smoke for about 15 minutes per side. Grill: 180 °F
3. While the pineapple is smoking, combine 1/4 cup water and sugar in a saucepan over low heat, stirring constantly, until sugar is dissolved. Pour syrup into a large bowl and set aside.
4. When the pineapple is done cooking, cut each slice into eight or so wedges and add the wedges to the bowl with the simple syrup, tossing to coat and cover.
5. Leave the mixture to macerate for at least 4 hours (or up to 24) in the refrigerator, stirring from time to time.
6. Strain the syrup into a clean bowl through a fine-mesh strainer and press on the pineapple with a ladle to extract as much liquid as possible. You can bottle and refrigerate the syrup for up to 4 days.
7. To make the cocktail: Combine the rum, lime juice, pineapple syrup, apricot brandy, and bitters

in a cocktail shaker or mixing glass. Fill with ice cubes and shake until cold.
8. Strain into a chilled cocktail glass. Garnish with a lime wheel and serve. Enjoy!

Smoke And Bubz Cocktail

Servings: 2
Cooking Time: 45 Minutes

Ingredients:
- 16 Ounce POM Juice
- 2 Cup pomegranate seeds
- 6 Ounce sparkling white wine
- 2 lemon twist, for garnish
- 2 Teaspoon pomegranate seeds

Directions:
1. Supply your smoker with wood pellets and follow the start-up procedure. Preheat the grill, with the lid closed, to 180° F.
2. For the Smoked Pomegranate Juice: Pour POM juice and a cup of pomegranate seeds into a shallow sheet pan. Smoke on the Traeger for 45 minutes. Pull off grill, strain, discard seeds and let sit until chilled. Grill: 180 °F
3. Add 1-1/2 ounces of the smoked pomegranate juice to the bottom of a champagne flute.
4. Add sparkling white wine, a few fresh pomegranate seeds and a lemon twist to garnish. Enjoy!

Traeger Old Fashioned

Servings: 2
Cooking Time: 60 Minutes

Ingredients:
- 2 orange
- 2 Cup cherries
- 3 Ounce bourbon
- 1 Ounce Smoked Simple Syrup
- 8 Dash Bitters Lab Apricot Vanilla Bitters

Directions:
1. Supply your smoker with wood pellets and follow the start-up procedure. Preheat the grill, with the lid closed, to 180° F.
2. While Traeger preheats, slice whole orange into wheels.
3. Place cherries on a small sheet pan and place in the Traeger. Place orange slices directly on the grill grate.
4. Smoke cherries for 1 hour and oranges for 25 minutes, depending on taste, before removing from the grill. Let oranges and cherries cool. Grill: 180 °F
5. Pour bourbon into glass, followed by Traeger Smoked Simple Syrup and bitters. Add ice and stir for 45 seconds or until drink is well-diluted.
6. Strain contents into new glass over fresh ice. Skewer orange wheel and add cherry for garnish. Enjoy!

Grilled Peach Sour Cocktail

Servings: 2
Cooking Time: 15 Minutes

Ingredients:
- 2 peach, sliced
- 2 Tablespoon sugar
- 1 1/2 Ounce Smoked Simple Syrup
- 4 Ounce bourbon
- 6 Dash Bitters Lab Apricot Vanilla Bitters
- 2 Sprig fresh thyme, for garnish

Directions:
1. Supply your smoker with wood pellets and follow the start-up procedure. Preheat the grill, with the lid closed, to 325° F.

2. Toss peach slices with granulated sugar and place directly on grill grate. Cook for 20 minutes or until grill marks form. Remove from grill and let cool. Grill: 325 °F

3. Place peaches and Traeger Smoked Simple Syrup into tin and muddle. Peaches should form about an ounce of juice during the muddling. Once completed, add remaining ingredients and shake.

4. Pour contents into glass over fresh ice and garnish with fresh thyme. Enjoy!

A Smoking Classic Cocktail

Servings: 2
Cooking Time: 60 Minutes

Ingredients:
- 2 Bottle Angostura orange bitters
- 10 sugar cubes
- 8 Ounce Champagne
- lemon twist

Directions:
1. Supply your smoker with wood pellets and follow the start-up procedure. Preheat the grill, with the lid closed, to 180° F.

2. For the Smoked Orange Bitters: In a small skillet, combine 1 bottle of Angostura orange bitters with a splash of water and 4 sugar cubes.

3. Place skillet on the grill grate and smoke for 60 minutes. Cool the smoked bitters and put back into the bottle. Grill: 180 °F

4. Add a sugar cube to each Champagne flute and soak the sugar cubes with the smoked bitters.

5. Add champagne and a lemon twist in a flute glass. Enjoy!

Grilled Hawaiian Sour

Servings: 2
Cooking Time: 15 Minutes

Ingredients:
- 2 Whole pineapple, trimmed and sliced
- 1/2 Cup palm sugar
- 3 Ounce bourbon
- 2 Ounce grilled pineapple juice
- 2 Ounce Smoked Simple Syrup
- 10 Ounce lemon juice
- 2 grilled pineapple chunk, for garnish
- 2 pineapple leaf, for garnish

Directions:
1. Supply your smoker with wood pellets and follow the start-up procedure. Preheat the grill, with the lid closed, to 350° F.

2. For the Grilled Pineapple Juice: Dust pineapple slices with palm sugar. Place directly on the grill grate and cook for 8 minutes per side. Grill: 350 °F

3. Remove from grill and let cool. Reserve a few pieces for garnish. Run remaining pineapple pieces through centrifugal juicer to extract juice.

4. To Make the Drink: Add bourbon, grilled pineapple juice, simple syrup and lemon juice to a cocktail strainer with ice. Shake vigorously. Double strain into a chilled coupe glass. Garnish with grilled pineapple chunk and pineapple leaf. Enjoy!

Grilled Blood Orange Mimosa

Servings: 4
Cooking Time: 15 Minutes

Ingredients:
- 3 blood orange, halved
- 2 Tablespoon granulated sugar
- 1 Bottle sparkling wine
- thyme sprigs, for garnish

Directions:
1. Supply your smoker with wood pellets and follow the start-up procedure. Preheat the grill, with the lid closed, to 375° F.
2. When the grill is hot, dip the cut side of the orange halves in sugar and place cut side down directly on the grill grate. Grill: 375 °F
3. Grill the oranges for 10-15 minutes or until grill marks develop. Grill: 375 °F
4. Remove from the grill and let cool at room temperature.
5. When cool enough to handle, juice the oranges and strain through a fine strainer removing any pulp.
6. Pour 5 oz of sparkling wine into each glass and top with 1 oz blood orange juice.
7. Garnish with a sprig of thyme. Enjoy!

Batter Up Cocktail

Servings: 2
Cooking Time: 60 Minutes

Ingredients:
- 2 whole nutmeg
- 4 Ounce Michter's Bourbon
- 3 Teaspoon pumpkin puree
- 1 Ounce Smoked Simple Syrup
- 2 Large egg

Directions:
1. Supply your smoker with wood pellets and follow the start-up procedure. Preheat the grill, with the lid closed, to 180° F.
2. Place whole nutmeg on a sheet tray and place in the grill. Smoke 1 hour. Remove from grill and let cool. Grill: 180 °F
3. Add everything to a shaker and shake without ice. Add ice, then shake and strain into a chilled highball glass.
4. Garnish with grated, smoked nutmeg. Enjoy!

Smoked Hot Buttered Rum

Servings: 4
Cooking Time: 30 Minutes

Ingredients:
- 2 Cup water
- 1/4 Cup brown sugar
- 1/2 Stick butter, melted
- 1 Teaspoon ground cinnamon
- 1/4 Teaspoon ground nutmeg
- ground cloves
- salt
- 6 Ounce Rum

Directions:
1. Supply your smoker with wood pellets and follow the start-up procedure. Preheat the grill, with the lid closed, to 180° F.
2. In a shallow baking dish, combine 2 cups water with all ingredients except for the rum and place directly on the grill grate. Smoke for 30 minutes. Grill: 180 °F
3. Remove from the grill and pour into the pitcher of a blender. Process until somewhat frothy.
4. Pour 1.5 ounces of rum each into 4 glasses. Split hot butter mixture evenly between the four glasses.
5. Garnish with a cinnamon stick and freshly grated nutmeg. Enjoy!

Smoked Plum And Thyme Fizz Cocktail

Servings: 2
Cooking Time: 60 Minutes

Ingredients:

- 6 fresh plums
- 4 Fluid Ounce vodka
- 1 1/2 Fluid Ounce fresh lemon juice
- 2 Ounce smoked plum and thyme simple syrup
- 4 Fluid Ounce club soda
- 2 Slices smoked plum, for garnish
- 2 Sprig fresh thyme, for garnish
- 8 Sprig thyme
- 2 Cup Smoked Simple Syrup

Directions:
1. Supply your smoker with wood pellets and follow the start-up procedure. Preheat the grill, with the lid closed, to 180° F.
2. Cut plums in half and remove the pit. Place the plum halves directly on the grill grate and smoke for 25 minutes. Grill: 180 °F
3. For the Plum and Thyme Simple Syrup: After 25 minutes, remove plums from the grill and cut into quarters. Add plums and thyme sprigs to 1 cup of Traeger Smoked Simple Syrup. Smoke the mixture for 45 minutes. Remove from grill, strain and let cool. Grill: 180 °F
4. Add vodka, fresh lemon juice and smoked plum and thyme simple syrup to a mixing glass.
5. Add ice and shake. Strain over clean ice, top off with club soda and garnish with a piece of thyme and slice of smoked plum. Enjoy!

Smoked Irish Coffee

Servings: 2
Cooking Time: 15 Minutes

Ingredients:
- 10 Ounce hot coffee
- 1/2 Cup heavy cream
- 1 Tablespoon sugar
- 2 Ounce Irish whiskey
- freshly grated nutmeg, for garnish (optional)

Directions:
1. Supply your smoker with wood pellets and follow the start-up procedure. Preheat the grill, with the lid closed, to 180° F.
2. Place the coffee and cream in separate shallow baking dishes and place both directly on the grill grate. Smoke for 10 to 15 minutes until the liquids pick up a slight smoke flavor. Grill: 180 °F
3. Remove from the grill and cool the cream. When the cream is cool, add sugar and whip in a stand mixer or by hand to soft peaks.
4. Pour the hot coffee into two mugs then add 2 ounces of whiskey to each.
5. Top with smoked whipped cream and finish with freshly grated nutmeg, if desired. Enjoy!

Smoked Grape Lime Rickey

Servings: 4
Cooking Time: 45 Minutes

Ingredients:
- 1/2 Pound red grapes
- 1/2 Cup plus 1 tablespoon sugar
- 1/2 Cup water
- 1 limes, sliced
- 2 limes, halved
- 1 Tablespoon sugar
- 1 L lemon lime soda

Directions:
1. Supply your smoker with wood pellets and follow the start-up procedure. Preheat the grill, with the lid closed, to 180° F.
2. Rinse grapes well and place in a shallow baking dish. Combine 1/2 cup sugar and water and stir until sugar dissolves. Pour over grapes.

3. Place the baking dish directly on the grill grate and smoke for 30 to 40 minutes until grapes are tender. Grill: 180 °F
4. Remove from the grill and pour entire contents of the baking dish in a blender. Puree on high until smooth then pass the mixture through a fine mesh strainer.
5. Increase Traeger temperature to 350°F. Grill: 350 °F
6. Toss the lime slices and lime halves with 1 tablespoon sugar and place directly on the grill grate. Cook for 15 to 20 minutes or until grill marks develop. Remove from grill and set slices aside. When cool enough to handle, juice grilled lime halves. Grill: 350 °F
7. To build the drink, fill a pint glass with ice. Pour in 1-1/2 ounce grilled lime juice, 1-1/2 ounce smoked grape syrup and top off with soda. Garnish with grilled lime slice. Enjoy!

Traeger Smoked Daiquiri

Servings: 2
Cooking Time: 25 Minutes

Ingredients:
- 2 limes, sliced
- 2 Tablespoon granulated sugar
- 3 Ounce Rum
- 1 Ounce Smoked Simple Syrup
- 1 1/2 Ounce lime juice

Directions:
1. Supply your smoker with wood pellets and follow the start-up procedure. Preheat the grill, with the lid closed, to 350° F.
2. Toss the lime slices with granulated sugar and place directly on the grill grate. Cook 20-25 minutes or until grill marks form. Remove from grill and cool. Grill: 350 °F
3. In a mixing glass add rum, Traeger Simple Syrup, and fresh lime juice. Add ice to the mixing glass and shake. Strain contents into a chilled glass.
4. Garnish with a grilled lime wheel. Enjoy!

Fig Slider Cocktail

Servings: 2
Cooking Time: 15 Minutes

Ingredients:
- 2 peach, halved
- 4 oranges
- honey
- sugar
- 2 Teaspoon orange fig spread
- 1 Ounce fresh lemon juice
- 4 Ounce bourbon
- 3 Ounce honey glazed grilled orange juice

Directions:
1. Supply your smoker with wood pellets and follow the start-up procedure. Preheat the grill, with the lid closed, to 325° F.
2. Pit the peach and cut in half. Cut one of the oranges in half. Glaze the peach and orange cut sides with honey and set directly on the grill grate until the honey caramelizes and fruit has grill marks. Grill: 325 °F
3. Cut the second orange into wheels and coat with granulated sugar on both sides. Place directly on the grill grate and cook 15 minutes each side or until grill marks form. Grill: 325 °F
4. In a mixing tin, add grilled peaches, bourbon, orange fig spread, fresh lemon juice and honey glazed orange juice.
5. Shake vigorously to blend the juices and fig spread. Strain over clean ice. Garnish with grilled orange wheel. Enjoy!

Smoked Berry Cocktail

Servings: 2
Cooking Time: 15 Minutes

Ingredients:
- 1/2 Cup strawberries, stemmed
- 1/2 Cup blackberries
- 1/2 Cup blueberries
- 8 Ounce bourbon or iced tea
- 2 Ounce lime juice
- 3 Ounce simple syrup
- soda water
- fresh mint, for garnish

Directions:
1. Supply your smoker with wood pellets and follow the start-up procedure. Preheat the grill, with the lid closed, to 180° F.
2. Wash berries well, spread them on a clean cookie sheet and place on the grill. Smoke berries for 15 minutes. Grill: 180 °F
3. Remove berries from grill and transfer to a blender. Puree berries until smooth then pass through a fine mesh strainer to remove seeds.
4. To create a layered cocktail, pour 2 ounces of berry puree in the bottom of a glass. Next, pour 2 ounces of bourbon or iced tea over the back of a spoon into the glass, then 1/2 ounce lime juice and 1/2 ounce simple syrup, top with soda water and ice. Finish with mint or extra berries for garnish.
5. Repeat the same process for 3 more servings. Enjoy!

Grilled Peach Mint Julep

Servings: 2
Cooking Time: 45 Minutes

Ingredients:
- 2 Whole peach
- 4 Ounce whiskey
- 2 Cup sugar
- 4 Tablespoon pink peppercorns
- 20 Whole fresh mint leaves, plus more for garnish
- 2 lime wedge, for garnish
- 4 Ounce bourbon

Directions:
1. For the Grilled Whiskey Peaches: cut peach into slices, then soak peach slices in whiskey in the refrigerator for 4 to 6 hours.
2. For the Pink Peppercorn Simple Syrup: In a shallow pan, combine sugar, 1 cup water and pink peppercorns.
3. Supply your smoker with wood pellets and follow the start-up procedure. Preheat the grill, with the lid closed, to 180° F.
4. Cook syrup down on the grill for 30 minutes, or until desired smoke flavor has been reached. Remove from the grill. Grill: 180 °F
5. Increase Traeger temperature to 350°F and preheat. Place the whiskey peach slices directly on the grill grate and cook 10 to 12 minutes or until peaches soften and get grill marks. Grill: 350 °F
6. To make the Julep: Muddle 1/2 ounce Pink Peppercorn Simple Syrup with 10 fresh mint leaves and 4 slices of grilled whiskey peaches.
7. Add crushed ice over the rim of the glass. Pour bourbon over the crushed ice and stir. Garnish with 1 large sprig of mint and fresh lime. Enjoy!

Smoking Gun Cocktail

Servings: 2
Cooking Time: 45 Minutes

Ingredients:
- 2 Jar vermouth soaked cocktail onions
- 3 Ounce vodka
- 1 Ounce dry vermouth

Directions:
1. Supply your smoker with wood pellets and follow the start-up procedure. Preheat the grill, with the lid closed, to 180° F.
2. To make the smoked onion vermouth: Pour jar of vermouth soaked cocktail onions onto a shallow sheet pan. Smoke for 45 minutes. Remove from grill and set aside to chill. Grill: 180 °F
3. To make the cocktail: Add vodka, 1 teaspoon liquid from the smoked onions and dry vermouth to a mixing glass. Shake and strain into a chilled martini glass.
4. Garnish with smoked cocktail onions on a skewer. Enjoy!

Smoked Salted Caramel White Russian

Servings: 4
Cooking Time: 20 Minutes

Ingredients:
- 16 Ounce half-and-half
- salted caramel sauce
- 6 Ounce vodka
- 6 Ounce Kahlúa

Directions:
1. Supply your smoker with wood pellets and follow the start-up procedure. Preheat the grill, with the lid closed, to 180° F.
2. Pour the half-and-half in a shallow baking dish and place directly on the grill grate. In another shallow baking dish, pour 2 to 3 cups of water and place on the grill next to the half-and-half.
3. Smoke both the half-and-half and water for 20 minutes. Remove from the grill and let cool. Grill: 180 °F
4. Place the half-and-half in the fridge until ready to use. Pour the smoked water into ice cube trays and transfer to the freezer until completely frozen.
5. Separate the smoked ice cubes into four glasses. Drizzle the salted caramel sauce around the inside of the glass.
6. Pour 1-1/2 ounce vodka and 1-1/2 ounce Kahlúa into each of the glasses and top with the smoked half-and-half. Enjoy!

BEEF LAMB AND GAME RECIPES

Smoked Meatball Egg Sandwiches

Servings: 4
Cooking Time: 25 Minutes

Ingredients:
- 3/4 Cup Breadcrumbs
- 2 Cloves Garlic, Minced
- 1 & 1/2 Lb. Ground Chuck
- 1 Jar Of Your Favorite Marinara Sauce
- 1 Large Eggs
- ¼ Cup Onion
- ¼ Cup Parsley, Minced Fresh
- ½ Tsp Pepper
- 1 Tbsp Chop House Steak Seasoning
- Provolone Cheese, Sliced
- ½ Tsp Salt
- Shredded Mozzarella Cheese
- 4 Sub Rolls Or Baguettes (6"), Sliced
- 2 Tbsp Worcestershire

Directions:
1. In a larger mixing bowl, combine the ground chuck, onions, garlic, Chop House Steak seasoning, salt, pepper, fresh parsley, Worcestershire, and egg. Add the breadcrumb mixture and parmesan cheese to the bowl and fold it into meat until well combined.
2. Supply your smoker with wood pellets and follow the start-up procedure. Preheat the grill, with the lid closed, to 400° F. If you're using a gas or charcoal grill, set it up for medium high heat and add your cast iron pan to the grill to warm up.
3. Roll the meat mixture into balls about 1 ½ inches wide, roughly the size of golf balls. Place meatballs into the cast iron skillet. Cook for 15 minutes or until meatballs are fully cooked and beginning to brown.
4. Pour full jar of marinara into the cast iron pan and gently stir to coat meatballs. Let simmer for 10-15 minutes.
5. Tear off four sheets of aluminum foil and place a sliced bun in the center of each. Divide the meatballs with sauce among the rolls. Top each roll with provolone cheese slices and mozzarella, and wrap entire sandwich tightly in foil. Return to the grill and cook an additional 10 minutes or until cheese is melty and bread has toasted. Serve immediately and enjoy!

Dry Brined Texas Beef Ribs By Doug Scheiding

Servings: 8
Cooking Time: 360 Minutes

Ingredients:
- 2 (9-12 Lb) Uncut Prime Or Choice Beef Short Ribs
- Kosher Salt
- Worcestershire Sauce
- Prime Rib Rub
- Blackened Saskatchewan Rub
- 8 Ounce Apple Juice, For Spritzing
- 8 Ounce Beef Broth

Directions:
1. Purchase a package of uncut short ribs from your favorite grocer or butcher store – recommended Prime or Choice quality. Usually 9-12 lbs for 2 racks of 4 bones each for 8 total.
2. Trim as much fat as possible from the top of the ribs with a sharp knife. Remove the

membrane from the bottom of each rack of 4 bones.

3. Sprinkle with kosher salt for the dry brine and wrap in plastic wrap for at least 6 hours or overnight in your refrigerator.

4. Supply your smoker with wood pellets and follow the start-up procedure. Preheat the grill, with the lid closed, to 275° F.

5. Wipe the excess salt mixture from the top of the ribs. Coat with a light amount of Worcestershire sauce before putting on a medium coat of Traeger Prime Rib.

6. Follow with a lighter coat of Traeger Saskatchewan rub. Spritz with apple juice and let set for 15-20 minutes.

7. Place on the Traeger with the thicker portion of the ribs (if applicable) to the back of the grill.

8. Smoke the ribs for 4-5 hours with a light spritz every 30 minutes to keep moist until internal temperature reaches approximately 180°F or the color has a nice deep char. Grill: 275 °F Probe: 180 °F

9. Like a brisket, take the ribs off the grill and wrap in 2 sheet of heavy duty foil along with 4 oz of broth for each rack of ribs.

10. Place back on the smoker for another 1 to 1-1/2 hours until internal temperature of the meat is around 203°F. Remove and cut. Serve immediately. Enjoy! Grill: 275 °F Probe: 203 °F

Beef Tenderloin With Tomato Vinaigrette

Servings: 6
Cooking Time: 40 Minutes

Ingredients:
- 1 Whole (1-1/4 to 1-1/2 inch thick) beef tenderloin steaks
- 1 Bottle Prime Rib Rub
- 2/3 Cup extra-virgin olive oil
- salt and pepper
- 1 Teaspoon fresh thyme
- 6 Whole plum tomatoes
- 1 Teaspoon Thyme, minced
- 2 Tablespoon balsamic vinegar

Directions:
1. Supply your smoker with wood pellets and follow the start-up procedure. Preheat the grill, with the lid closed, to 450° F.

2. Tuck the thin end of the tenderloin underneath the roast and secure it with butcher's string. Rub the meat with olive oil and season it with the Prime Rib Rub or salt and pepper. Place the meat on a rack in a shallow roasting pan.

3. Roast in the preheated Traeger for 20 minutes. Adjust the heat to 350F. Roast 20 minutes longer, or to desired degree of doneness (130F for rare; 145F for medium; 155F or higher for well-done). Grill: 350 °F

4. Let rest for 5 minutes before slicing thinly. (If serving cold, thoroughly chill the tenderloin before slicing.) Garnish with sprigs of thyme.

5. To make the vinaigrette, combine the tomatoes, olive oil, balsamic vinegar, and thyme leaves in a blender jar or food processor; puree until smooth. Season to taste with Traeger Prime Rib Rub or salt and pepper.

6. Transfer to a gravy boat and serve with the tenderloin. (Best served the day it's made.)

Irish Pasties

Servings: 4
Cooking Time: 20 Minutes

Ingredients:
- 1 Pound Roast Beef, cubed & browned

- 4 Whole Potatoes, cooked & cut into 1/2" cubes
- salt and pepper
- 1 Piecrust
- milk
- 2 Cup Beef Gravy

Directions:

1. Supply your smoker with wood pellets and follow the start-up procedure. Preheat the grill, with the lid closed, to 425° F.

2. Mix the beef, potatoes, salt, and pepper in a large mixing bowl. Unroll the piecrust, and cut in half. Put a good amount of filling in each half, fold over, and seal shut. Brush with a little milk.

3. Place on a greased basking sheet, and poke a few holes in the top of each pasty. Bake for 16-20 minutes, or until the crust is golden brown. Grill: 425 °F

4. Remove from the Traeger, brush with butter, and serve with gravy. Enjoy!

Smoked Tri-tip

Servings: 4
Cooking Time: 300 Minutes

Ingredients:

- 1½ pounds tri-tip roast
- Salt
- Freshly ground black pepper
- 2 teaspoons garlic powder
- 2 teaspoons lemon pepper
- ½ cup apple juice

Directions:

1. Supply your smoker with wood pellets and follow the start-up procedure. Preheat the grill, with the lid closed, to 180°F.

2. Season the tri-tip roast with salt, pepper, garlic powder, and lemon pepper. Using your hands, work the seasoning into the meat.

3. Place the roast directly on the grill grate and smoke for 4 hours.

4. Pull the tri-tip from the grill and place it on enough aluminum foil to wrap it completely.

5. Increase the grill's temperature to 375°F.

6. Fold in three sides of the foil around the roast and add the apple juice. Fold in the last side, completely enclosing the tri-tip and liquid. Return the wrapped tri-tip to the grill and cook for 45 minutes more.

7. Remove the tri-tip roast from the grill and let it rest for 10 to 15 minutes, before unwrapping, slicing, and serving.

Bbq Burnt End Sandwich

Servings: 2
Cooking Time: 480 Minutes

Ingredients:

- 1 point cut brisket
- Beef Rub
- 1/2 Cup beef broth
- 1 Cup Texas Spicy BBQ Sauce
- 4 Slices Monterey Jack cheese
- 4 burger buns

Directions:

1. Supply your smoker with wood pellets and follow the start-up procedure. Preheat the grill, with the lid closed, to 250° F.

2. Trim excess fat off brisket point. Season brisket point liberally with Traeger Beef rub.

3. Place brisket point directly on the grill grate. Cook until it reaches an internal temperature of 170°F, approximately 4 to 5 hours. Grill: 250 °F

4. Remove brisket from grill and cut into 1-inch cubes. Add the beef broth to the pan with the cubed brisket. Cover pan with aluminum foil.

5. Place pan in grill and cook for 90 minutes. Grill: 250 °F

6. Remove the foil and add Traeger Texas Spicy BBQ sauce. Stir and put back on the grill, uncovered, for an additional 45 minutes. Remove from grill. Grill: 250 °F

7. Top each bun with the burnt ends, cheese, and additional BBQ sauce. Enjoy!

Citrus Grilled Lamb Chops

Servings: 4 - 6

Cooking Time: 15 Minutes

Ingredients:

- 2 Tablespoons Chophouse Steak Seasoning
- 4 Finely Garlic Clove, Minced
- 2 Pounds Thick Cut Rib Chops Or Lamb Loin
- Juice From 1/2 Lemon
- Juice From 1/2 Lime
- ¼ Cup Olive Oil
- 3 Tablespoons Orange Juice
- ¼ Cup Red Wine Vinegar

Directions:

1. In a mixing bowl, whisk together all the ingredients and 2 tbsp Chophouse Steak. Place the lamb chops in a glass baking pan and pour the marinade over the top. Flip the chops over a few times to make sure that they are completely coated.

2. Cover the glass pan in aluminum foil and allow the lamb chops to marinade for 4-12 hours. Once the meat has finished marinating, drain off the excess marinade and discard.

3. Supply your smoker with wood pellets and follow the start-up procedure. Preheat the grill, with the lid closed, to 400° F. If you're using a gas or charcoal grill, set it up for medium high heat. Grill the chops for 5-7 minutes per side, then lower the temperature to 350°F or medium heat, and flip and grill for another 5-7 minutes.

4. Remove the lamb chops from the grill, cover in foil, and allow to rest for 5 minutes before serving.

Sweet Heat Burnt Ends

Servings: 8-10

Cooking Time: 360 Minutes

Ingredients:

- 1 (6-pound) brisket point
- 2 tablespoons yellow mustard
- 1 batch Sweet Brown Sugar Rub
- 2 tablespoons honey
- 1 cup barbecue sauce
- 2 tablespoons light brown sugar

Directions:

1. Supply your smoker with wood pellets and follow the start-up procedure. Preheat the grill, with the lid closed, to 225°F.

2. Using a boning knife, carefully remove all but about ½ inch of the large layer of fat covering one side of your brisket point.

3. Coat the point all over with mustard and season it with the rub. Using your hands, work the rub into the meat.

4. Place the point directly on the grill grate and smoke until its internal temperature reaches 165°F.

5. Pull the brisket from the grill and wrap it completely in aluminum foil or butcher paper.

6. Increase the grill's temperature to 350°F and return the wrapped brisket to it. Continue to cook until its internal temperature reaches 185°F.

7. Remove the point from the grill, unwrap it, and cut the meat into 1-inch cubes. Place the cubes in an aluminum pan and stir in the honey, barbecue sauce, and brown sugar.

8. Place the pan in the grill and smoke the beef cubes for 1 hour more, uncovered. Remove the burnt ends from the grill and serve immediately.

Smoked Pheasant

Servings: 4-6
Cooking Time: 240 Minutes

Ingredients:
- 1 gallon hot water
- 1 cup salt
- 1 cup packed brown sugar
- 2 (2- to 3-pound) whole pheasants, cleaned and plucked
- ¼ cup extra-virgin olive oil
- 2 tablespoons onion powder
- 2 tablespoons freshly ground black pepper
- 2 tablespoons cayenne pepper
- 1 tablespoon minced garlic
- 2 teaspoons smoked paprika
- 1 cup molasses

Directions:

1. In a large container with a lid, combine the hot water, salt, and brown sugar, stirring to dissolve the salt and sugar. Let cool to room temperature, then submerge the pheasants in the brine, cover, and refrigerate for 8 to 12 hours.

2. Remove the pheasants from the brine, then rinse them and pat dry. Discard the brine.

3. Supply your smoker with wood pellets and follow the start-up procedure. Preheat, with the lid closed, to 250°F.

4. In a small bowl, combine the olive oil, black pepper, cayenne pepper, onion powder, garlic, and paprika to form a paste.

5. Rub the pheasants with the paste and place breast-side up on the grill grate. Close the lid and smoke for 1 hour.

6. Open the smoker and baste the pheasants with some of the molasses. Close the lid and continue smoking for 2 to 3 hours, basting with the molasses every 30 minutes, until a meat thermometer inserted into the thigh reads 160°F.

7. Remove the pheasants from the grill and let rest for 20 minutes before serving warm or cold.

Naked Juicy Lucy Burgers With Special Sauce

Servings: 4
Cooking Time: 40 Minutes

Ingredients:
- 2lb (1kg) ground beef (80/20), preferably chuck, well chilled
- 1 tbsp Worcestershire sauce or liquid aminos
- 6oz (170g) grated Cheddar, pepper Jack, or another melting cheese
- coarse salt
- freshly ground black pepper
- for the sauce
- ¼ cup reduced-fat mayo
- ¼ cup yellow mustard
- ¼ cup ketchup
- ¼ cup Heinz 57 sauce
- 2 tbsp sweet pickle relish
- for serving
- sliced tomatoes

- sliced sweet onions
- lettuce leaves
- cooked bacon strips
- Pickles

Directions:

1. Supply your smoker with wood pellets and follow the start-up procedure. Preheat the grill, with the lid closed, to 225° F.
2. In a small bowl, make the sauce by combining the ingredients. Transfer the sauce to a serving bowl. Cover and refrigerate until ready to use. (Leftover sauce will keep for several weeks.)
3. Place the ground beef in a large bowl and add the Worcestershire sauce. Wet your hands with cold water and lightly mix. Divide the mixture into 8 equal-sized balls. Flatten each ball into a round patty.
4. Place 4 patties on a rimmed sheet pan. Mound an equal amount of cheese in the middle of each patty, leaving a meat border. Place a patty on top of each cheese mound. Rewet your hands with cold water and press and pinch the edges of patties together to form a tight seal. (You don't want the cheese to leak out.) Season on both sides with salt and pepper.
5. Place the patties on the grate and smoke for 30 minutes. Transfer the burgers to a clean plate.
6. Raise the temperature to 450°F (232°C). Return the burgers to the grate and sear them until the burgers reach an internal temperature of 160°F (71°C), about 3 to 4 minutes per side, turning once.
7. Transfer the burgers to a platter and let rest for 3 minutes. Serve with the special sauce and the suggested accompaniments.

Philly Cheese Onion Steaks

Servings: 6
Cooking Time: 45 Minutes

Ingredients:

- 2 Green Bell Pepper, Sliced
- 6 Hot Dog Bun(S)
- 2 Cups Mozzarella Cheese, Shredded
- 1 Quart Mushroom
- 1 Onion, Sliced
- Pepper
- Salt
- 2 Thick Steak, Flank

Directions:

1. Supply your smoker with wood pellets and follow the start-up procedure. Preheat the grill, with the lid closed, to 250° F.
2. Season both sides of your steaks with salt and pepper to your liking. We're going to reverse sear these steaks, so place on the grates of your preheated Grill. You'll want to cook the steaks until the internal temperature reaches 130°F (for medium-rare). Follow these internal temperatures if you'd like to cook your steak more/less done:
3. Rare: 125°F
4. Medium Rare: 130°F
5. Medium: 140°F
6. Well Done: 160°F
7. If you're cooking your steaks medium rare, it will take around 45 minutes depending on how thick the steaks are.
8. While the steaks are cooking, slice up the onion, mushrooms, and peppers thinly and sauté until soft.
9. When the steaks have reached your desired internal temperature, remove steaks from the grill and let them rest for 15 minutes. In the meantime, open up your flame broiler and crank up the grill

to HIGH. Sear each side of the steak for about 1 minutes each.
10. Rest steaks again for 10 minutes.
11. Slice steak thinly, combine with the sautéed vegetables and fill a hot dog bun generously with the mixture.

Sweetheart Steak

Servings: 2
Cooking Time: 12 Minutes

Ingredients:
- 1 (20 Oz) Boneless Strip Steak Or Rib Steak, Butterflied Into Heart Shape
- 2 Teaspoon Jacobsen Salt Co. Pure Kosher Sea Salt
- 2 Teaspoon black pepper
- 2 Tablespoon Raw Dark Chocolate, finely chopped
- 1/2 Tablespoon extra-virgin olive oil

Directions:
1. Draw a large heart on a piece of cardboard, shape to size of meat selected. Cut out cardboard heart shape, then trim meat into heart shape.
2. Combine all ingredients on the cut steak.
3. Supply your smoker with wood pellets and follow the start-up procedure. Preheat the grill, with the lid closed, to 450° F.
4. Grill steak for 5 to 7 minutes per side, or until you've reached desired doneness. Remove from grill. Let rest for 5 minutes. Enjoy!

Cornish Game In Mandarin Glaze

Servings: 4
Cooking Time: 45 Minutes

Ingredients:
- 2 Tablespoon onion powder
- 1 Tablespoon granulated garlic
- 1 Tablespoon Jacobsen Salt Co. Pure Kosher Sea Salt
- 1 Tablespoon ground ginger
- 5 Whole Cornish game hens
- 15 Sprig fresh thyme
- 2 Large oranges, quartered
- 2 Tablespoon olive oil
- 1 Bottle (12 oz) mandarin orange sauce

Directions:
1. Supply your smoker with wood pellets and follow the start-up procedure. Preheat the grill, with the lid closed, to 375° F.
2. Combine onion powder, granulated garlic, Jacobsen Salt and ground ginger.
3. Remove the hens from the packaging. Remove any giblets from each cavity and pat them dry with a paper towel.
4. Place 4 to 5 sprigs fresh thyme into each cavity, along with 1 orange wedge.
5. Sprinkle each bird with the spice mixture, then rub with olive oil. Tie the legs together with butcher's twine.
6. Place the game hens on the Traeger and cook for 20 minutes. Grill: 375 °F
7. After 20 minutes, brush each hen with mandarin glaze. Let them cook an additional 20 minutes and brush again with the glaze. Grill: 375 °F
8. Cook until hens have reached an internal temperature of 160°F. Enjoy! Grill: 375 °F Probe: 160 °F

Beef Brisket With Chophouse Steak Rub

Servings: 12
Cooking Time: 480 Minutes

Ingredients:
- As Needed, Chop House Steak Rub
- 1, 10 To 12 Lb Whole Beef Brisket

Directions:
1. Supply your smoker with wood pellets and follow the start-up procedure. Preheat the grill, with the lid closed, to 250° F.
2. While the grill is heating up, trim your brisket of excess fat, score the meat against the grain and season with Chop House Steak Rub or your favorite seasoning.
3. Place your brisket on the grates, fat side up and cook for 7-8 hours or until the internal temperature reaches 190°F. If the meat is not probe tender, keep cooking until your temperature probe can easily slide into the meat with little to no resistance.
4. Remove from the grill and allow to rest for 20-30 minutes.
5. Slice against the grain and enjoy!

Fajita Style Mexican Hot Dogs

Servings: 4
Cooking Time: 10 Minutes

Ingredients:
- 1 Green Bell Pepper, Sliced
- 1 Package Hot Dog Bun(S)
- 1 Package High Quality Ballpark Hot Dog(S)
- 1 Tbsp Olive Oil
- 1 Tsp Beef And Brisket Rub
- 1 Yellow Bell Pepper, Sliced
- 1 Yellow Onion, Sliced

Directions:
1. Supply your smoker with wood pellets and follow the start-up procedure. Preheat the grill, with the lid closed, to 350° F.
2. In a large bowl, toss the peppers and onions with the olive oil and Beef and Brisket Rub. Place the vegetables on the mesh grilling basket.
3. Remove from the grill and assemble the hot dogs. Top the buns with a hot dog and a generous scoop of the onion and pepper mixture. Serve immediately.

Spiced Lamb Burgers With Tzatziki

Servings: 4
Cooking Time: 10 Minutes

Ingredients:
- 1½lb (680g) ground lamb or a mixture of lamb and beef, well chilled
- 1/3 cup grated red onion
- 1 to 2 garlic cloves, peeled and minced
- 2 tbsp chopped fresh dill or fresh mint
- 1 tsp ground cumin
- ½ tsp ground cinnamon
- ½ tsp crushed red pepper flakes (optional)
- extra virgin olive oil
- coarse salt
- freshly ground black pepper
- for the tzatziki
- 1/3 hothouse cucumber, unpeeled and coarsely grated
- coarse salt
- 1½ cups plain Greek yogurt, drained
- 1 to 2 garlic cloves, peeled
- 1 tbsp freshly squeezed lemon juice or white distilled vinegar
- 1½ tbsp extra virgin olive oil

- 1 tbsp chopped fresh dill or fresh mint

Directions:

1. Supply your smoker with wood pellets and follow the start-up procedure. Preheat the grill, with the lid closed, to 450° F.

2. Make the tzatziki by placing the cucumber in a sieve and lightly sprinkle with salt. After 15 minutes, rinse with cold running water. Drain and then squeeze the cucumber dry with paper towels. Transfer the cucumber to a large bowl. Add the yogurt, garlic, and lemon juice. Stir to mix. Season with salt to taste. Transfer to a serving bowl. Set aside. Just before serving, drizzle with the olive oil and scatter the fresh dill over the top.

3. In a large bowl, combine the lamb, red onion, garlic, dill, cumin, cinnamon, and red pepper flakes (if using). Wet your hands with cold water and mix thoroughly but gently. (Try not to overhandle the meat.) Form the meat into 4 patties of equal size, each about ¾ inch (2cm) thick. Use your thumbs to make a shallow depression in the top of each burger. Lightly oil the outsides of the burgers with olive oil. Season with salt and pepper.

4. Place the burgers on the grate and grill until the internal temperature reaches 160°F (71°C), about 4 to 5 minutes per side, turning once.

5. Transfer the burgers to a platter. On a separate platter, place thinly sliced red onions, thinly sliced tomatoes, thinly sliced cucumbers, crumbled feta, and Kalamata olives. Serve with the tzatziki and pita bread.

Flavour Bbq Brisket Burnt Ends

Servings: 6-8
Cooking Time: 420 Minutes

Ingredients:
- 1 Brisket Point
- Georgia Style BBQ Sauce (Mustard Base)
- As Needed Chop House Steak Rub

Directions:

1. Supply your smoker with wood pellets and follow the start-up procedure. Preheat the grill, with the lid closed, to 250° F.

2. Place your brisket on the grates, cook for 6 to 7 hours or until the internal temperature reaches 190°F

3. Remove from the grill and cut into 1-inch cubes. Toss brisket cubes with seasoning and your favorite BBQ sauce into a pan.

4. Place the pan in the grill for 2 hours, stirring half-way through.

Bourbon Beef And Pork Meatballs

Servings: 4
Cooking Time: 25 Minutes

Ingredients:
- 1 cup cubed stuffing, unseasoned
- 2 , beaten eggs
- 3 garlic cloves, minced
- 1 lb ground beef
- 1 lb. ground pork
- 2.5 cups maple bourbon glaze
- 1 tbsp sweet heat rub
- 1, grated yellow onion
- 2 tbsp milk

Directions:

1. Supply your smoker with wood pellets and follow the start-up procedure. Preheat the grill, with the lid closed, to 350° F. If using a gas or charcoal grill, set it up for medium heat.

2. Put the stuffing in a food processor and pulse to process into small crumbs. Pour the crumbs out into a mixing bowl, then add the onion, garlic, eggs, milk, and Sweet Heat. Let the mixture sit for 10 minutes, then add the ground meat. Using your hands, combine the mixture together until fully incorporated.

3. Form mixture into 2 ounce balls and place on cast iron skillet, evenly spaced apart.

4. Transfer skillet to preheated grill and cook for 15 minutes, then generously glaze with sauce. Cook an additional 5 minutes, then glaze again and cook for 2 more minutes.

5. Remove meatballs from grill and serve hot with remaining sauce (about ⅓ cup).

Roasted Elk Jalapeno Poppers

Servings: 10
Cooking Time: 15 Minutes

Ingredients:
- 4 elk steaks
- 1 Cup Worcestershire sauce
- 1 Cup lime juice
- 1 Cup soy sauce
- 20 jalapeño peppers
- 10 Pieces bacon
- 12 Ounce herb & garlic flavored cream cheese, room temp
- Raw Honey

Directions:
1. Mix the lime juice, Worcestershire, and soy sauce together in a large bowl. Alternatively you can pour the ingredients directly into a large ziplock bag. Add sliced steak, cover and let sit for 4-6 hours to overnight.

2. Supply your smoker with wood pellets and follow the start-up procedure. Preheat the grill, with the lid closed, to 350° F.

3. Remove the steak from the marinade and thinly slice into bite-sized pieces so they are approximately the same width and length as the jalapeños.

4. Cut the jalapeños in half lengthwise; remove seeds and center membrane and set aside.

5. Cut the bacon in half crosswise. Set aside.

6. Spoon cream cheese equally into all jalapeño halves.

7. Lay one slice of marinated elk on top of each jalapeño. Wrap each jalapeño popper with one piece of bacon and secure with a toothpick if needed.

8. Place on grill, cut side up for 10-15 minutes or until elk is cooked and jalapeños are tender and lightly charred.

9. Remove from the grill and optionally drizzle with honey before serving. Enjoy!

Smoked Pot Roast Brisket

Servings: 6
Cooking Time: 240 Minutes

Ingredients:
- 1 Coca-Cola, can
- 1 Heinz Chili Sauce, bottle
- 1 Dry Onion Soup Mix, package
- 4 Pound flat cut beef brisket

Directions:
1. Mix the Coke, Heinz chili sauce (you can find it in the condiment aisle of the grocery store) and dry onion soup mix in a bowl.

2. You'll want to trim the fat on the brisket, leaving only about 1/4 inch on top.

3. Put the brisket into a large baking pan and pour the Coke-chili sauce mixture over top. (If you use a larger piece of brisket, or the whole brisket you may need to double the sauce mixture.)
4. Supply your smoker with wood pellets and follow the start-up procedure. Preheat the grill, with the lid closed, to 300° F.
5. Put the pan of brisket on the grill and cook for 3 to 4 hours or until the brisket is tender. (Stick a fork in it and when it twists with little effort, it's ready!) Grill: 300 °F
6. Let the brisket rest, covered in its juices for 30 minutes to an hour before you slice her up and serve.

Beef Caldereta Stew

Servings: 12
Cooking Time: 240 Minutes

Ingredients:
- 1/2 cup cheddar cheese, grated
- 2 lbs, cut into 1 1/2" cubes chuck roast
- 4 garlic cloves, chopped
- 1 tsp kosher salt
- 2 tbsp olive oil
- 2 large yukon gold potatoes
- 5 chopped serrano peppers
- 2 tbsp tomato paste
- 2 cups tomato sauce
- 2 cups water

Directions:
1. Place beef in a cast iron skillet, then transfer to smoking cabinet. Make sure that the sear slide and side dampers are open, then supply your smoker with wood pellets and follow the start-up procedure. Preheat the grill to 375° F, to ensure the cabinet maintains temperature between 225°F and 250°F (If you're cooking on a different Pellet Grill, set the temperature to 225°F).
2. Smoke beef for 1½ hours, then turn cubed beef, and smoke an additional 1½ hours.
3. Place cast iron Dutch oven on the grill, over flame. Add olive oil, potatoes, and carrots. Cook for 3 to 5 minutes, stirring occasionally. Then add leeks and garlic and cook for 2 minutes, until fragrant.
4. Remove skillet from smoking cabinet and add beef pieces to potato mixture.
5. Add tomato sauce, tomato paste, water, and serrano peppers. Bring to a boil, then cover with lid. Set temperature to 275°F, and allow stew to simmer for 1 hour, until beef and potatoes are tender.
6. Add liver and cheese, and gently stir to combine, until the sauce thickens and cheese has melted.
7. Add bell peppers and olives. Stir, cover and cook an additional 2 minutes. Season with salt, and serve hot.

Garlic Prime Rib Roast

Servings: 8
Cooking Time: 30 Minutes

Ingredients:
- 2 tsps black pepper
- 10 cloves garlic, minced
- steak seasoning
- 2 lbs prime rib roast
- 2 tsps salt

Directions:
1. Supply your smoker with wood pellets and follow the start-up procedure. Preheat the grill, with the lid closed, to 400° F.

2. Rub roast garlic, salt, pepper and some Chop House Steak Rub.

3. Insert meat thermometer sideways into the center of the roast so that the shaft is not visible, avoiding fat and bone.

4. Cook in a closed grill, maintaining constant heat, until the thermometer reads 145°F(63°C) for medium-rare for about 50 minutes, or cook until desired doneness.

5. Remove roast to cutting board; tent with foil for 5 to 10 minutes. Serve with mashed potatoes and asparagus on the side.

Grilled Lemon Skirt Steak

Servings: 1-2
Cooking Time: 5 Minutes

Ingredients:
- 2 Cloves Garlic, Chopped
- 1 Lemon, Juice
- 2 Tablespoons Mustard, Grainy
- 1/4 Cup Olive Oil
- 2 Tablespoons Java Chophouse Seasoning
- 2 Pounds Skirt Steak, Trimmed
- 1 Tablespoon Worcestershire Sauce

Directions:
1. In a small bowl, mix together the Java Chophouse Seasoning, oil, garlic, lemon juice, and Worcestershire. Generously rub the mixture all over the skirt steak and allow to marinate for 45 minutes.

2. Supply your smoker with wood pellets and follow the start-up procedure. Preheat the grill, with the lid closed, to 400° F.

3. Grill the skirt steaks for 3-5 minutes on each side or until the steak is done to the desired degree of doneness.

4. Remove the steaks from the grill and allow to rest for 5 minutes before slicing and serving.

Traeger Smoked Salami

Servings: 8
Cooking Time: 480 Minutes

Ingredients:
- Pound Ground Sirloin
- 1 Tablespoon Morton Tender Quick Home Meat Cure
- Tablespoon Worcestershire sauce
- 1 Tablespoon ground black pepper
- 2 Teaspoon mustard seeds
- 1 Teaspoon red pepper flakes
- 1 Teaspoon black peppercorn
- Teaspoon honey

Directions:
1. Plan ahead! This recipe requires overnight time. In a large glass bowl combine the beef, curing salt, Worcestershire, pepper, mustard, red pepper flakes, and peppercorns. Gently distribute the ingredients through the meat.

2. Cover with plastic wrap and refrigerate for 1 day.

3. After the meat has cured for 1 day, lay two pieces of long plastic wrap on top of each other on your work surface. Overturn the meat directly into the middle of the plastic wrap. Form the meat into a long log shape.

4. Pull the plastic wrap around one side and smooth out the edges of the log. Use even pressure across the length to work out any bubbles. Pull the plastic wrap tightly around the other side and overlap the edges of the wrap to create a tight seal. Roll the sausage forward and back with both hands. Once you have the sausage fairly uniform in width, tightly twist the ends of

the plastic wrap. Return to the refrigerator for 1 day.

5. Supply your smoker with wood pellets and follow the start-up procedure. Preheat the grill, with the lid closed, to 180° F.

6. Unwrap the sausage and drizzle with the honey. Place directly on the grill grate, close the lid and smoke for 6-8 hours or until the internal temperature of the sausage reads 170°F with a meat thermometer. Probe: 170 °F

7. Allow the sausage to cool completely before slicing and serving. Enjoy!

Printed in the USA
CPSIA information can be obtained
at www.ICGtesting.com
LVHW080443081124
795985LV00009B/1657